THE FIRST
100
YEARS

Ruttger's

1898 · CENTENNIAL CELEBRATION · 1998

Bay Lake Lodge

The Ruttger Song

Aimee Ritchie—1930s

There's a place we all know.
It's the place we all go.
It's Ruttger's Bay Lake Lodge.
The days full of sunshine.
The nights sweet and cool.
It's a kind of life that
Comes once, so that you'll
Come again every year, and
You'll meet those so dear
Where you played, fished, or golfed
Day or night.

When the time comes next year
We will all meet you here –
At Ruttger's Bay Lake Lodge!

THE FIRST 100 YEARS

Ruttger's
1898 CENTENNIAL CELEBRATION *1998*
Bay Lake Lodge

By Mae Ruttger Heglund

ISBN 0-9661599-1-8
© 1998 Ruttger's Bay Lake Lodge

PUBLISHED BY

EVERGREEN PRESS

1863 Design Drive
Baxter, MN 56425
(218) 828-6424

Acknowledgements

Many thanks to the following people for their contributions in the making of this book. Their suggestions and input have added much to the content.

1. Carl A. Zapffe for his written permission to use information from his book OLDTIMERS II, sent to us before his untimely death.
2. Judy Knieff for her valuable advice about how to prepare a book for publication.
3. Jack and Ann Ruttger for their valuable suggestions and changes in order to make a more interesting book and also for written materials.
4. Chris Ruttger, Jane Ruttger Bobich, Ruby Treloar, Gretchen Klein, and Joe and Sharon Simons for their writings and information. Shirlee Ruttger Bates for information and suggestions, and Buzz (Max J.) Ruttger for the use of family pictures and recipes of Grandmother Josephine Ruttger.
5. Thanks so much to Chef Terry Dox for sharing some of his very tasty recipes with us.
6. A special thanks to Kay Bargen for her input.
7. Finally, thanks so much for the special help given us by the publishers, Evergreen Press of Brainerd, especially Aaron Hautala for his hard work and creativity.

In the book we have included many of the pictures that are on the walls here and there at the resort which seem to be of interest to visitors. We have also presented some of the past history of the area as that was where Ruttger's Bay Lake Lodge had its start.

My family and I appreciate all of the work done by Annette Kittock in preparation of this historical publication. She has done much editing and has given valuable advice on how to make this a more appealing book.

Annette Kittock.

Mae Ruttger Heglund

Ruttger's Bay Lake Lodge, P.O. Box 400, 15000 Tame Fish Lake Road, Deerwood, MN 56444
Phone: (218) 678-2885 • 800-450-4545 • Fax: (218) 678-2864 • website: www.ruttgers.com

CONTENTS

RUTTGER'S BAY LAKE LODGE: THE FIRST 100 YEARS

The Farm That Wouldn't Cooperate

By Steve Keillor, previously printed in *Lake Country Journal*

"The farm is being conducted on cooperative principles. . . . Nobody expects to get rich on it."

With those words, James S. Rankin, a former Minneapolis newspaper editor, described to the *St. Paul Pioneer Press* reporter his new cooperative farming colony on the north shore of Bay Lake in Crow Wing County. The year was 1886, and the national labor union, the Knights of Labor, was drawing headlines around the country for its phenomenally rapid growth. A member of the Pillsbury family donated money for this cooperative farm, one of the Knights' many cooperative efforts. Rankin left the *Minnesota Mirror* in order to organize it.

The Twin Cities Knights recruited two machinists, a brass finisher, an editor, a printer—twenty people in all—to settle at Bay Lake in a cooperative experiment that drew national attention. Among the settlers was Joseph Ruttger of Minneapolis, hired as a machinist to revive the abandoned sawmill formerly used by an early settler named Ashael Bennett. Ruttger built a house on Bay Lake Island (now known as Malkerson Island), not amidst the other settlers, which seems like an individualistic move but was apparently accepted by the other members of the cooperative.

Northern Pacific Railroad sold a Knights-led land company 253 acres of land that was to be cleared and farmed by these members of the Pioneer Cooperative Company. Picking the wild raspberries, strawberries, and blueberries that grew there in abundance was a simple enough task. Pasturing sheep on the island and making maple sugar did not seem arduous.

Clearing the forest was another matter. The abandoned sawmill on the property could only cut lumber after the trees were down. They were too late in sowing their oats that spring of 1886.

Knowing the value of publicity, the ex-editor made regular visits to the editor of the *Brainerd Dispatch*: "Our crops are coming along finely," he said on one such trip. But no more than twenty acres had been cleared by December 1887. When Rankin boasted to the *Minneapolis Star* that month that the colony was doing fine, it was the last straw for one colonist. "We were obliged to buy most of our stuff," he reported—certainly a mark against this experiment in self-sufficiency.

Several disgruntled colonists complained of Rankin's poor management as the main difficulty. None too subtly, the *Star* reported, "All the men who are able to do any work have left the colony and only Mr. Rankin and his family are now on the grounds." One colonist "went so far as to tear down his house and cart it off the colony's land."

Rankin failed to make his editorials on cooperative farming materialize in the forest. But Joseph Ruttger would find a better, more leisurely use for the land. Now, Ruttger's golf course occupies it. Anyone for cooperative best-ball golf? 𝓡

Steve Keillor is a historian and the author of two books on Minnesota history. He is currently writing a book on Minnesota cooperatives for the Minnesota Historical Society.

Mae Ruttger Heglund.

Introduction

I have been chosen to be in charge of doing the historical record of Ruttger's Bay Lake Lodge, as well as a brief history of my beloved Bay Lake area and our family. I am Mae Ruttger Heglund, the oldest of three children born to Alec and Myrle Ruttger, and have spent much of my life connected with the resort. Members of the Alec Ruttger family and friends of the family have contributed information for this "labor of love." Ruttger's has reached what we have decided is the centennial year—though it was not started as a resort, just a place for people to stay and eat when they came to rest, fish, and escape the heat. Our family and other persons connected with Ruttger's Bay Lake Lodge thought it would be a good idea to write down a record of background history as a means of preserving the past and also as a memorial to our Centennial Year in 1998. ®

Mae looking over the photos that are to be placed in the book.

Chapter One
Early Bay Lake History

1899 - Fishing is terrific!
Original Ruttger house, formerly the Colony Store. The tent was one of the first guest accommodations.

For many years the only summer tourists of the Bay Lake area were the Indians who paddled and portaged among the bodies of water for their fishing and hunting. They were mainly based by Mille Lacs Lake, but also used Bay Lake and surrounding lakes and streams for transportation. In the mid-1770s, the Mille Lacs residents were Sioux. By the early 1800s, the Sioux (or Dakota) were gone, because the Ojibwe (or Chippewa) had driven them into the southern part of the state. This takeover of the ancient Sioux homeland in northern and central Minnesota by the Ojibwe took place during the great Indian Revolution of the 18th century. This was at the same time as the American Revolution. The French had supplied arms and steel traps to the Ojibwe fur harvesters who then moved farther and farther west until they were pushing into Sioux country. In 1736, the Sioux murdered 19 Frenchmen on what we now call Massacre Island in Lake of the Woods. Warfare began about 1739 when the Ojibwe quietly climbed the Sioux sod houses at Mille Lacs just before dawn and dropped bags of gunpowder into their fire holes. In three days the great Sioux strong-

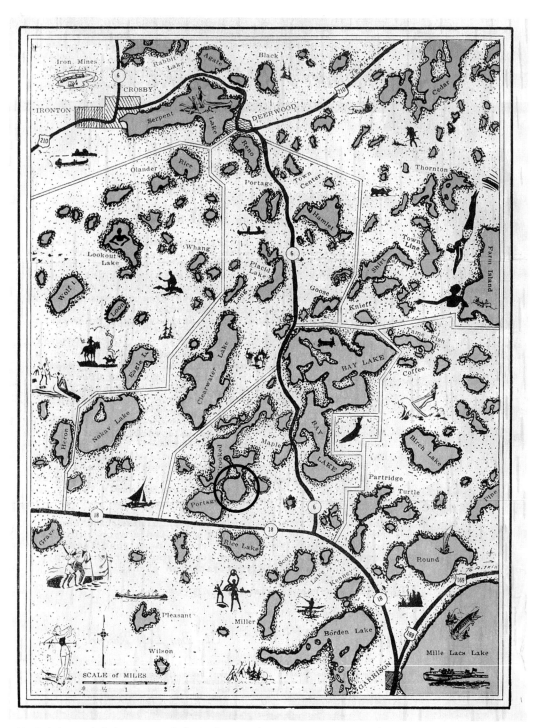

Hanks Lake, circled above, named after William Hanks (see page 13) is part of the Crooked Lake chain.

"Battle Point on Bay Lake," a painting by Sarah Thorp Heald, represents a historic battle between the Sioux and Ojibwe nations almost 200 years ago. The painting is on permanent display at the Crow Wing County Courthouse.

hold on Mille Lacs was abandoned, and the survivors fled down the Rum River.

The Sioux tried to dislodge the Ojibwe into the 1800s and were rapidly repossessing their favorite community locations. One of these ancient Sioux villages must have been on or close to Bay Lake. There is a tale that has been told that near the opening of the 19th century a Sioux war party returned to Bay Lake, and a band of Ojibwe was living on what we now call Battle Point, in commemoration of the event. At dawn, the Sioux in their canoes stealthily worked north from a canoe-portage route and approached the rear or southerly side of the "big island" on Bay Lake, out of sight of the Ojibwe. When they were a little more than a half-mile from the tip of the peninsula, as

the story is told, an Ojibwe young woman was down on the shore where she spotted the Sioux warriors approaching and ran to warn her people in camp, but it was too late. Through their surprise attack, the Sioux were able to kill the tribe living on the point. This has been memorialized by a

The Pine Family.

large oil painting of the maiden by the lakeshore, beautifully done by Sarah Thorp Heald, which may be found in the Crow Wing County Courthouse.

According to Carl Zapffe in his Oldtimers II book, explorers found as many as 24 Indian villages on Mille Lacs Lake, with one particularly close to Bay Lake. Canoe passageways ran from Mille Lacs

David Archibald, first Bay Lake white settler.

Lake to Borden, then into either Kinney or Miller Lakes, then into Scott, Rice, Portage, Hanks, and finally Bay Lake. The other passageway was Mille Lacs to Round, to Turtle, then Partridge and then into the south tip of Bay Lake. The passageway from Bay Lake to Deerwood was Milem to Placid Lake, then Portage, Reno, and then Serpent Lake at Deerwood. Bay Lake was a very centralized location for lake travel in those days. A north-northwesterly route off what became Ruttger's property brought them through Milem or Goose Lake to Shirt and Hamlet, then on to Portage Lake with its portage to Reno and Serpent Lakes (Deerwood).

Bay Lake is about 4 miles long and has approximately 25 miles of shoreline. It has many bays, islands, peninsulas, and hills, which make for a great many beautiful spots. The name Bay Lake came from the

Indian name of Sissebagamah which meant "lake of many bays."

According to Mr. Zapffe, there were two full-blooded Ojibwe Indians by the name of John Pine and William Hanks, who both had graduated from Carlyle College and homesteaded land "whiteman style," even though this had been their own homeland. Hanks Lake was named after the family of William Hanks. The main reason for the beginning of homesteading at Bay Lake was the laying of the tracks of the Northern Pacific Railroad during the fall of 1870 and the founding of the little station stop called Withington in early 1871. The name was changed to Deerwood later to eliminate confusion with the station at Worthington. Financial failure of the Northern Pacific in 1872 and 1873 pretty much stopped homesteading throughout

The Bay Lake School.

the 1870s. When the company revitalized in 1879, homesteading started to increase. S. H. Reif had completed maps of Bay Lake in 1883 and again in 1886, and they showed pioneers that were living there at that time. Some of the names listed on the north end of Bay Lake are: David

PROGRAM
Bay Lake, Minn. July 4, 1930.

9:00 A. M.—GOLF TOURNAMENT
Closes 4:00 P. M. Low medal play. Prizes for all classes of players. Entrance fee, 50 cents.

9:30 to 12:00 Noon—TRAP SHOOTING
Prizes to be divided money. R. R. Graham in charge.

10:00 A. M.—PARADE AND RACING EVENTS
Led by Ironton Boys' Band, Prof. William Knuppel, director; Ivan Ringstad of St. Paul, in charge.

10:30 A. M.—TENNIS TOURNAMENT
Finals at 4:00 P. M. Players furnish own ball. F. G. Mayberry in full charge. Entrance fee 50 cents. Prizes, divided money.

10:30 A. M.—HORSESHOE PITCHING TOURNAMENT
Closes at 2:00 P. M. Entrance fee 50 cents. Prizes, divided money. Hugo Knieff in charge.

11:00 A. M.—SPEAKER

12:30 P. M.—BASEBALL GAME
Deerwood vs. Ore Diggers. Prize $25.00. Winners take all.

1:00 P. M.—BATHING BEAUTY CONTEST
At Green Lantern. Mrs. Maudie Ruttger in charge.

2:00 P. M. SPEED BOAT RACES
Entrance fee $2.00. Class "B" prizes: First, $25; second, $15; third, $10. Class "C" prizes: first $25; second, $15; third, $10. Class "F" prizes: first, $25; second, $15; third $10.
FREE FOR ALL PRIZES—first, $40; second, $25; third, $15; fourth, $10. Fred Schwanke in charge.

Surf board races after speed boat races. Shortest time winner. Time added when not standing up. Prizes: first, $6; second, $4. Bucking barrel contest. All day events. No entrance fee. One dollar per minute to the one who can stand on barrel without assistance in water waist deep.

Joy Riding on Speed Boat for visitors. All day events.
Tickets sold at docks. Adults 25c; children under 12 years 15c for trip around speed boat course. Adults 50c, children under 12 years, 25c for trip around island.

Open Air Concert by Ironton Boys' Band
Prof. Wm. Knuppel, director. Also comic German Band lead by "Hub" Coffin, Detroit, Mich.

Deerwood to Bay Lake was by the Indian water route via Reno, Portage, and Long to Bay Lake, and from there to Mille Lacs. Adams, along with David and Robert Archibald, cut a path connecting Deerwood to Bay Lake. It is generally believed that David Archibald was the first white settler in Bay Lake.

In 1884, the county commissioners established the Bay Lake precinct and named John Milem, David Archibald, and Nick Newgard as judges. The voting place was at Mr. Milem's place of residence on Milem Lake, just west of Bay Lake. Bay Lake boomed in 1884—it was established as a voting precinct, the Bay Lake school was built in District 11, and a post office was established with Ashael Bennett as postmaster. The school was built on the John Milem homestead property and was organized May 6, 1884. John Milem had donated one acre of property for the school. Before the fall term, a frame building was ready to be used, made from lumber sawed at Torrey's mill and put together by John Milem, Heinrich Knieff, David Archibald, Godfrey Christensen, Victor Peterson, and two Downey men. The school term lasted five months—two in the fall and three in the spring. Furniture for the schoolroom consisted of a long table with benches on

Archibald, C. G. and Nicolas Christensen, John Milem, A. Bennett, and James D. Torrey. According to some records, Bay Lake did not have permanent white settlers until 1882 when Cuyler Adams came to the Deerwood area. He said one of the first things he had in mind was to clear a trail to Bay Lake; the only other way to travel from

H.H. Ziegler and Mae Ruttger Heglund in his arms. July 4, 1930.

each side, with a small table and chair for the school ma'am. Two boys were assigned each day to bring a pail of water from the spring below Archibald's cabin on the lakeshore of Bay Lake. Uncle Bill Ruttger said the first teacher he remembered was Mr. Lurch. The first day of school he took a razor strap and swung it around saying he would use it if he had to. One student didn't come back for the rest of the year.

The settlement received the name of Bay Lake in 1894. Some of the above-mentioned names were carried down in the history of the area—there is a Milem Lake for John Milem and an area named Bennettville, which is six miles east on County Road 14, (Ruby Treloar's home) for A. Bennett, for instance. The first Fourth of July celebration was held at Bay Lake in 1895—an event that was very popular with area people. I found an article in the <u>Deerwood Enterprise</u> dated June 6, 1930, telling of a big Fourth of July celebration that was planned. There were to be $400 in prizes which would be awarded to

4th of July at Bay Lake.

4th of July at Bay Lake.

H. H. Ziegler ("bride") in a mock wedding, 1930 in the Log Dining Room.

winners in sport events that included speed-boat races, surfboard races, baseball games, golf tournaments, horseshoe pitching, and tennis games. A band was engaged for the afternoon and many other attractions, besides those mentioned, were to be featured. The Bay Lake Sportsmen's Club was sponsoring the celebration with H. H. Ziegler of Junction City, Kansas, who was a member of the Bay Lake summer colony, in charge of the arrangements. They said all roads were to lead to Bay Lake, barring rain. The problems confronting the committee in charge were parking space and how to keep the highway open along the lake shore. Everybody within a radius of 50 miles was heading for Bay Lake, the paper said.

The large island off the southeasterly corner of "Ruttger Island" was homesteaded by A. F. Landstrom around 1900. Mr. Landstrom had very poor fortune. His wife died in childbirth leaving him with a son who later died of tuberculosis. After those two tragedies, Mr Landstrom turned the property over to the Swedish Evangelical Lutheran Church, and the island became known as "Church Island." Church services are still held there every Sunday during the summer.

By 1882, local building had created such a demand for lumber that James D. Torrey erected a sawmill on the northwest shore of Bay Lake, southwest from the Ruttger location. There were 12 families of

Musical Selection ---------Mr. and Mrs. Wilbur Hunt

Scenes From the Life of the North American Indians
lonial Days.
          Mr. Earl Archibald, Chairman

Massachusetts Colony—
    Scene I. Puritans at Home.
    Scene II. Puritans on Way to Church.
          Mrs. L. P. Hall, Chairman.

New York Colony—
    Short Talk by Mr. C. G. Christensen.
    Dutch Story by Chester Powers.
    Dutch Dance by the Young Folks.
    Holland's National Song.
        Mrs. Joseph Ruttger, Chairman.

5. William Penn's Colony—
    "A Pair of Scissors," by Five Quaker Dames.
        Miss Huseby, Chairman.

6. Early Pioneers and Explorers of the Mississippi Valley
nd Great Lakes Region.
      Mr. John Christensen, Chairman.

7. Virginia Colony—
    Playlet: 'Historical Virginians."
      Mr. Hugo Knieff, Chairman.

8. Closing Song: "We Are All Americans."

Schedule of entertainment at the Bay Lake schoolhouse. Grandma Josie played her Steinway piano at many events.

Ojibwe, including chieftains Nokay and Kabasheboi, living on the point across from the new mill. The point later became known as Indian Point.

During that same summer, another sawmill was erected by Asa Bennett a couple hundred yards east of the later Ruttger location. He was the man for whom Bennettville on Farm Island Lake in Aitkin County would later be named, as mentioned earlier. A. A. Miller Sr. later took over the sawmill that Torrey started, as well as the Indian Point property. Uncle Bill Ruttger told about logging in the area. He said he remembered of a million feet of timber taken off the "big island." A lot of lumber was shipped out of the area, and some was kept for building purposes. They floated timber on the lake, then oxen and horses pulled cart loads of logs across mainland trails to Deerwood where they were shipped by rail.

According to Zapffe, two developments transpired in 1883 that greatly affected subsequent Bay Lake history. First was the thorough survey of the area by the S. H. Reif party, and second was the arrival of Henry Knieff. Henry (Heinrich) had married Louisa Wasserzieher on October 12, 1872, in Nauvoo, Illinois. She and their family moved to Bay Lake with him. Louisa was sister to Josephine, who eventually married Joseph Ruttger.

The North Bay Lake schoolhouse was located where the tennis courts are— north of the gift shops. It was used as a one-room schoolhouse until about 1932. The building was also used as a community type of church and as a meeting place for neighborhood activities, such as the Sportsmen's Club (also a card-playing group). My Aunt

Rosie (Mrs. Max) Ruttger remembered the good times they had using the building for plays they put on, as well as parties. The building was also used for Ladies Aid, a group of ladies who got together to have monthly meetings, sales of craft items they had made, as well as a reason to get together as neighbors. The Willing Workers Ladies Aid was affiliated with the Methodist Church, as the Methodist pastor of the area was the one that gave weekly services. However, many of the ladies were really members of other denominations. They attended mostly to be a part of the social group. The same pastor served the Crosby and Deerwood churches as well. I remember attending services and other activities in the school building. There was a small coat room where you entered. Then you would go through a door into the main part which had many windows, and there were many blackboards on the walls that were not covered by windows. There was a large wood stove at the far corner, a very small kitchen which had been added later, no running water, a large hand pump outside, and two little houses out back (pretty cold in the winter).

From May 10, 1886, until the latter part of 1887, an experiment was tried in Township 45, Range 28. Incorporated Pioneer Cooperative Company was granted a charter to buy and hold land to exemplify cooperative methods of production and distribution. Incorporators were James S. Rankin, Wm. N. Bethel, Chas. W. Shephard, Joseph Ruttger, Augustine J. Bacon, J. H. Rankin, and A. Stafford. This co-op was backed by the Knights of Labor, and they obtained under contract a tract of 253 acres of land from the Northern Pacific railroad to be used for colonization. They set up a sawmill for which Joseph Ruttger was hired to be an engineer. This was the sawmill Bennett had used and was located to the east of where the main lodge is now located.

Each member filed on a homestead. Joe homesteaded the island. In 1894, he bought mainland property from J. S. Rankin and moved from the island, because the ice was too thin to travel on in the fall and spring. According to Alec, Grandpa Joe kept the island for a while, and the family continued farming there for a period of time. He said they took a horse over to cultivate the land. They put the cultivator in a boat and had the horse swim behind. As he remembered, Grandpa Joe gave his equity in the island to a Mr. Seavey in return for his labor in building the big house about 1901. Later the island was listed on the 1913 Atlas as being owned by Cuyler Adams. (The Cuyuna Range area was named for Cuyler and his dog, Una.)

In November of 1929, the island was presented to the Minneapolis Area Boy Scout Council by Frank S. Gold, president of the council, who had purchased it from Adams. This 54-acre island was then known as the Isle of Pines. The Scouts decided to transfer their camping activities elsewhere in 1955, and Les Malkerson, married to Betty Gold, daughter of Frank Gold, purchased his Quit Claim Deed from them. He and his family have lived there seasonally ever since.

The old Ruttger home stood on the southeasterly part of the island, a couple hundred yards east of the narrow neck. There is a small cabin at this time built over the Ruttgers' root cellar—it is the only cabin there with a root cellar. ✏

(see photo next page)

Joe, Josie, and Mr. Gold at the Ruttger homestead on the Bay Lake Island, 1930. Homestead had been built before 1890.

Chapter Two
How Tourism Began with Joseph and Josephine

Railroad lines came to Deerwood, and this seemed to open up land to travelers. The coolness of the lakes in central Minnesota was a big attraction and Bay, Reno, and Serpent Lakes were very popular in this area. Grandpa Joe and Grandma Josie's hospitality and Josie's great cooking attracted visitors to stay—sleeping in tents,

Bay Lake Summer Resort

J. RUTTGER

Deerwood, Minn.

Ten Thousand Lakes of Minnesota Association

THIS HOTEL IS NOT RESPONSIBLE FOR LOSS OF MONEY OR JEWELS OR OTHER VALUABLES UNLESS DEPOSITED IN THE SAFE PROVIDED FOR THAT PURPOSE IN THE OFFICE

MAIL TO TEN THOUSAND LAKES OF MINNE-SOTA ASSOCIATION, SAINT PAUL, EACH WEEK   *1920*   Date_____

NAME	ADDRESS	ROOM	CHECK OUT	MODE OF TRANSPORTATION
Katherine Sullivan	Saint Joseph Mo.	19		Motored
Mr Mrs H McKnight	Cedar Rapids			
R.G. Stewart	Cedar Rapids Ia			
G. Linville	Cedar Rapids Ia	3		
Dr Mrs J.J. Curran	Oakland Ia.			Motored
Geo M Bethel Wife	Minneapolis			
Mr Mrs R Schayer	Ft Madison Ia			
Mr Mrs W Page Jr.	Chicago, Ill.		July 3, 1920	
Dorothy Kearns	Duluth, Minn			
J W Churchill	Cedar Rapids			
Mr D Kauffman	Saint Louis		July 31, 1920	Motored
Frank N Belong	St. Louis		July 31, 1920	
J. A. Canfield	Cedar Rapids			
Agnes K Tayling	Duluth Minn	"		
Lillian Wick		"		

This registration sheet is from 1920, when Ruttger's was called "Bay Lake Summer Resort."

The Kansas crowd.

haymows, and some on the banks of the lake to escape the heat in towns. There was no air conditioning in those days, so soon after the turn of the century people from Kansas and Missouri began to find the Bay Lake area. Reservation books from Ruttger's show some registering in the early 1900s. A portion of the north shore of Bay Lake is still called the "Kansas Colony" because of the many Kansas people who bought property and built summer homes there. The rail connections and buckboard service between Ruttger's home and the railroad station were good; thus the beginning of the Ruttger legacy.

The house that Joseph and Josephine had built later became the base for the present lodge building including the lobby where the bar is located, the upstairs where the accounting/management offices are, the basement now used for storage and the wine cellar, and the liquor room. The latter was Grandmother Josie's kitchen. Joe and his family operated a berry farm and a large onion patch on about 40 acres of land. This was the property that later became Ruttger's Bay Lake Lodge.

In Joseph Ruttger's obituary, in the Crosby paper, it stated that he and Josephine were married on October 31, 1890, and established the resort business at that time. I would wonder about that because they were living on the large island across from the resort until 1894. I would have thought that living on the island would be too limiting to have regular guests. Ruttger's Bay Lake Lodge has the reputation of possibly being the first resort in northern Minnesota. However, Lutsen on Lake Superior disputes that claim. For sure, Ruttger's has the distinction of being operated the longest by one family.

1901 porch of the Ruttger Big House. A quote from Mrs. Ed (Eva) Ruttger; "You could always see Mrs. Below and Miss Bryant sitting on the front porch in their long black skirts and white blouses."

The Story of Joseph and Josephine

Joseph Ruttger was born in Neuleiningen, Germany, on January 13, 1860, to John and Catherine Wolfe Rüttger. He was born into a family of seven sons and one daughter: Josef, Adam, Christian, Franz, Ludwig, Bernhard, Johannes, and Katharina. Joseph was a skilled machinist. He had taken his apprenticeship with a recognized member of the guild, and for several years had been traveling as a journeyman, going by foot from town to town, generally receiving free lodging but no pay.

Joseph left Germany to avoid the draft. He left Germany by boat through Holland. On October 30, 1881, at the age of 21, he arrived in the U.S. and found employment in Pittsburgh. Four months later he moved to Minnesota and found employment at the St. Paul Milwaukee Shop, a lathe factory. In the early spring of 1886, during noon hours, two men named J. S. Rankin and William Krech promoted northland living with the idea of starting a "colony" which would settle 253 acres of beautiful land in Minnesota's lake country recently obtained from the Northern Pacific Railroad. It was their plan to take over an existing sawmill in order to support themselves. With this enticement and the fact that he had contracted a lung ailment while working at the St. Paul shop, he left the city, and on April 26, 1886, he homesteaded the large island on Bay Lake which is located directly across from the present Ruttger's property. Joe served as steamboat engineer where he received stamps which could be traded in at the company store for food and other necessities. The company store stood just to the west of where the main lodge of Ruttger's now stands. There is record that Joseph

Joseph Ruttger, 1941.

served as road overseer and constable at one time, so it appears people must have taken many different roles in the new community.

When he left the city, the doctor who diagnosed his lung ailment gave him three months to live, which turned out to be very wrong. Joseph died on April 20, 1941, at St. Joseph's Hospital in Brainerd, at the age of 81. Funeral services were held at the resort, with Rev. Clara Wagner of Humboldt, former woman pastor of Bay Lake, and Rev. A. I. Gausman officiating, with burial in the

Josephine and Joseph's wedding photograph.

Bay Lake cemetery.

Josephine Wasserzieher came to Bay Lake from Nauvoo, Illinois, in 1889, in order to be a companion to her sister, Louisa Knieff, after the death of her husband, Henry, who had passed away on October 26, 1888. They lived a very short distance from where Joseph was living on the island. Joseph and Josephine soon met and fell in love. It was said that Joe would leave his home on the island in the morning, going by rowboat or sleigh, of course, taking his lantern with him so as to spend the day until after dark. Joseph and Josephine were married in the Knieff home on October 31, 1890. Alexander John was born to them in 1892 on the island. They moved to the mainland in 1894. They had five sons, one of whom died in infancy. The surviving sons were Alexander, Maximillian (Max), Edward, and William.

Josephine and first son, Alexander.

Joseph Ruttger was a very good-hearted person and had some characteristics that made for many stories that have carried down over the years. My Uncle George Mattson remembers when there were some bear cubs on resort property getting to be pretty good size. The mother had been killed, so the cubs were brought in and kept for a period of time. Grandpa liked to play with the cubs. One time he

Joseph's pet bears.

gave one of them a shove, and it in return gave him a cuff. Grandpa Joe's false teeth flew out of his mouth. The bear thereupon put the teeth in its mouth. Grandpa kicked the bear in the stomach and the teeth flew out. Grandpa then picked up the teeth and put them back into his mouth. He must have been a little too brusk at times, and once he got into a fisticuff and got a black eye. When someone asked him where he got the black eye, he swore he bumped into a harness peg. Grandpa Joe loved to talk. He would ask someone if they had heard a certain story. If they had heard it he would say: "I'll tell you again lest you forget." And, of course, if you had not heard it he would tell you. He had a distinct German accent, as he came to this country when he was grown. Alec said that he remembered times when his father, Joe, sang in his deep bass voice in the little schoolhouse/church, and he actually heard the windows rattle. I remember him singing "Come to the Church in the Wildwood," and was impressed, even though I was very young at the time. A story told by Alec about his father: "One Sunday Joseph was waiting anxiously for the pastor to finish a long prayer so he could rush to Deerwood to meet guests on the train. The preacher's pulpit was near the door so Joe could not get by until the prayer was fin-

Joseph in work clothes.

ished. He decided not to wait any longer and tiptoed up to the pulpit, tapped the parson on the shoulder telling him, "I wouldn't mind if you could cut the prayer short as I have to hurry to Deerwood with my team to meet some guests on the train."

One last story about Grandpa Joe told to us by Uncle Bill Ruttger: The Scofields lived where the Hall property is now or just west of Battle Point. Grandpa wasn't on very good terms with Mr. Scofield. One time Joe had taken a load of wood to town to sell. On the way back he met Mr. Scofield on the road with his load of wood turned over. Grandpa and Mr. Scofield were not speaking and hadn't been

for some time. Grandpa stopped and helped him load the wood back on his wagon without saying a word, then got back on his own wagon and went on still without a word.

Uncle Bill said that Joe's first car was a 1913 Ford which he bought from a man named Roth. He said Joe drove quite a lot. The roads in the area were not very good so it took about one-half hour to go to Deerwood in the old cars. He said the road between Hamlet and Portage Lakes, which

Joseph and Josephine.

passed by what later became Cedarbrook Manor and eventually Heartland Skating, was only passable for one vehicle at a time in those days. They had to stop to listen as to whether or not they could hear anybody coming before going on.

Josephine Wasserzieher Ruttger was born in Nauvoo, Illinois, on October 27, 1860. Her parents were Edward Adolph and Otillia Neitzert Wasserzieher. Josephine was one of eleven children—three boys and eight girls, two of whom died dur-

Josephine Wasserzieher Ruttger, an accomplished pianist.

Otillia Neitzert and Edward Adolph Wasserzieher at their golden anniversary.

Mormon denomination to Nauvoo when they headed west out of New York in 1838. Six years later, Joseph Smith was killed by a mob, and in 1846 the Mormons set out on the historic trek which ended in Salt Lake City. Smith had been a friend of the Wasserziehers according to Gilbert Wasserzieher who has done much family background research.

Alec, William, Max, and Ed (in front).

ing infancy. The surviving members of the family were Otto, Mary, Louisa, Hermina, Ottilie, Maximillian, Anna, Ernest, and Josephine. The family lived on property left by the Mormons who had planted many fruit trees and vineyards. Their family became one of the leading producers of grapes and wine in Nauvoo.

Nauvoo is located on the Mississippi River, about 45 miles north of Quincy. Joseph Smith led his followers of the future

Joseph and Josephine by the piano.

Josephine was a very busy lady. She had her piano shipped to Bay Lake from Nauvoo, and she gave piano lessons to many in the area. She and Joseph were very good about having neighbors in, and they had good times with music from the piano to accompany the singing that went on. Many neighbors came from miles around to the Ruttger home, traveling with

The Ruttger Boys at the Post Office.

"German Love Song" that they were noted for. Josephine's Steinway piano may be seen at the Crow Wing County Historical Museum in Brainerd in a room that has other family memorabilia in it.

Josephine was noted for her good cooking, and she was the beginning of a tradition at Ruttger's. Josephine was appointed as postmistress of the Bay Lake Post Office in 1895 and held that position until 1909 at which time mail route delivery was begun. The Post Office was connected to the Ruttger home on the west side and can be seen in the picture below.

their sleds pulled by teams of horses to spend the long winter evenings socializing and singing. The four Ruttger boys sang songs accompanied by the booming bass voice of their father, Joseph. The older people would tell about how they always insisted that Joe and Josie perform the old

One publication I found stated that there were five "resorts" in the Bay Lake area in the early years: Youngs, Soules, Archibalds, Sissebagamah, and Ruttgers. I would guess these were more likely sleeping rooms in their homes that they rented out

Ruttger's Bay Lake—the cornerstone of the present lodge.

Young's Bay Lake.

Archibald's Bay Lake.

Soule's Bay Lake.

Sissebagamah Bay Lake.

and possibly haymows and tents to stay in as well.

As mentioned, Joseph and Josephine had not intended to go into the tourism business; it just seemed to evolve due to demand. Before the last spike was driven connecting Deerwood to Brainerd, fishermen were getting off at the end of the line in Deerwood. About the year 1896, Mr. Lichleiter, a livery man from Deerwood just five miles away, kept boarders. He started bringing fishermen to the Ruttger home where Joe would rent them a boat in the morning. When they returned to shore in the evening, tired and hungry, they pleaded with Josie for supper. She fed them with home-grown vegetables and home-butchered and cured meat. They then asked for a place to sleep. Some slept in horse-blankets in the hayloft and in tents that

The livery.

were purchased as a temporary solution for housing summer guests. In the morning they were again looking for food and would probably fish for the day. The livery would then deliver them back to catch the midnight train at Deerwood.

Eventually, Josephine began charging

for meals, and this was the start of the tourist business. Running a resort was difficult in those days. They had to have a team of horses, a buggy, plenty of kerosene for lamps, stacks of firewood, lots of food from gardens and slaughter, lots of labor cooking and baking on wood-burning stoves, and they needed to cut ice in the winter to be used as refrigeration. The ice was stored in sawdust in an icehouse. It was used to keep fish fresh and also hauled out to be used in an icebox for preservation of food in the house. Alec remembered that they harvested a lot of cabbage and made sauerkraut in huge crocks, preparing enough for their own use and also to give to neighbors. Bill remembered the Penny Muffins his mother made, and German food that was served— one being homemade liverwurst.

The boys worked in the gardens where they raised a lot of onions as well as other vegetables. Dad told of one time Grandpa spanked Max in the garden. Max said, "Why are you spanking me? I didn't do anything." To which Grandpa replied, "That's why I'm spanking you."

They also raised raspberries and blackberries which Joe used to take to the train in Deerwood, sometimes getting home very late at night.

Making maple syrup.

The family tapped maple trees on their property in the spring in order to make their own pancake syrup as well as maple candy. The maple sap was boiled down at their "sugar bush," a place set up to cook the water out of the sap in order to end up with syrup and sugar. This was not usually done in the house as the sugary steam would coat surfaces, making a mess.

A friend, Mae, and Jack in front of the barn.

Later the Ruttgers built a building they named "fishermen's house." It was a two-story building with ten compartments or rooms. The downstairs had a living room where the fishermen could sit and spin their yarns and tell fishing tales in front of a fireplace. The upstairs sleeping rooms were reached by an outside stairway. For five dollars a person per week they could have a room, meals, and a boat. Some slept in the dormitory and others in tents. The guests furnished the fish, policed the grounds on certain days, made their own beds, etc. The Ruttgers provided their own vegetables, berries, pork, eggs, chickens, milk, cream, and churned their own butter. Each fall the family gathered to butcher hogs raised on table scraps and corn and to gather a year's vegetables to place in their root cellar.

Max, Alec, Joseph, Josephine, Ed, and Bill.

Alec and Leroy Zeitelman playing horseshoe in front of the fishermen's house.

About all they bought were staple groceries. No wonder they could charge such a low rate. As time went on, people were hired to help with yard work, clean rooms, wait on tables, and do other jobs that became too much for the family to keep up with. I have seen canceled checks that were made in payment to local young girls that were hired, as they said, to clean, deliver water to rooms, and carry out and empty the little china buckets that were kept under the beds. We received information from Frank Wolf of Northfield, Minnesota, telling us that his grandparents Frank H. and Helen Bryant Below came to Ruttger's in 1901, bringing with them their three children: Helen Dorcas (his mother), Bryant, and Frank, Jr. -- Helen Below's sister, Margaret Bryant, and her parents, James Ray McCorkle Bryant, and his wife, Helen Margaret, also came with them. They had heard of Ruttger's on Bay Lake from an

Hen House (girls' dorm for employees) formerly fishermen's house.

acquaintance named Forbes. From 1901 through 1927, this group or part of it spent some of their summers at Ruttger's, Soule's, or at the Young's. A Mr. Dawson also sometimes was in residence with the families, as he was a friend of Margaret. As of this writing, Frank's niece, Peggy Blistain, and her two daughters are working at Ruttger's, so the family is still in evidence. Ruttger's place was advertised mainly by word of mouth, and, gradually, families started to come. In the early days most of the tourists came from Brainerd, Aitkin, Duluth, Kansas, and Missouri. The main interest was fishing, and large numbers were caught. One of the advantages of the Ruttger property was that it had a southern exposure so the cold winds were off-shore to the back. During one par-

The Below clan with H. H. Ziegler sitting in front.

ticular hot spell there were 75 people that came from Brainerd, Aitkin, and Deerwood just to be by the water and escape the heat. They sat by the lake all night to keep cool from the breeze over the water.

I found a letter among some of Joseph's things that was sent from the Minnesota Board of Health, dated October 28, 1912. They stated that the barn, chicken coop, and hog pen were located in a spot that drained into Bay Lake and that it would cause pollution. I was not aware that people would know about pollution in those days. I believe the barn was located on the top of a small hill, just to the east of the parking lot in front of the lodge. It was torn down and rebuilt on the spot where the riding stable would eventually be located. That barn burned in the 1930s.

An early Bay Lake group.

Joseph and Josephine Ruttger in the fishermen's house, 1912.

An aerial view of Ruttger's Bay Lake Lodge in 1935.

L to R: William, Alec, Joe, Max, Edward.

The Family of Joseph and Josephine

Alexander John Ruttger was born on the big island visible from the front of Ruttger's Lodge on September 12, 1892. He had a very active life and made many changes and advances during his management of Ruttger's Resort.

Maximillian Wilhelm Ruttger, or Max as he was known, was born on the mainland on September 15, 1894. He married Rose Scott on New Year's Eve, 1914. Max was the first of the brothers to pass on—he died on June 7, 1951. Max and Rosie operated the Bay Lake General Store from 1914 - 1930. They built a resort on Gull Lake in 1930 which they named Ruttger's

Pine Beach Lodge. They and their two sons, Don and Max Jr., operated the resort in the summers, and returned to their home at Bay Lake to live during winters. Their home was located next to the Bay Lake store in those years.

Edward Adolph Ruttger was born July 5, 1896. He married Eva Peddycoart, October 2, 1922. They had three children: Raymond, Shirlee, and David. Ed, Eva, and their family were involved in the resort business when they operated Ruttger's Sherwood Forest Lodge on Gull and Margaret Lakes between the years of 1934 and 1946. After selling the resort, Ed went

into the real estate business; his son, Raymond, joined his father in that business; and his grandson, Jim, is still carrying on the tradition. Ed passed away on December 31, 1982, and his lovely wife, Eva, on April 3, 1994.

William Joseph, the "baby" of the family was born on November 1, 1899. He married Maude White on April 29, 1923. They were blessed with two sons, one named Joseph and the other William, who died in infancy. Bill operated the Bay Lake Store from 1930 until 1936, at which time he and his family built and operated Ruttger's Shady Point Lodge on Whitefish Lake. Bill and Maude Ruttger operated Shady Point Lodge from 1936 to 1958.

Their son, Joe, his wife, Carol, and their three children ran the resort from 1958 to 1979, when it was sold. Joe and Carol both died before Maude and Bill, leaving a big void in the family. Maude died on January 21, 1992. Bill died at the age of 93 on December 19, 1992, at Whispering Pines Good Samaritan Center in Pine River, Minnesota. He had Parkinson's disease for many years and was not able to care for himself, though his mind remained sharp to the end. He had many stories to relate from past years and enjoyed reciting poetry that he had composed years before. Following are three poems that Bill recited for some of us while he was a resident at the nursing home.

Alec, Ed, and Bill Ruttger.

Poems by Bill Ruttger

My Mother

I thank the Lord for her creation
She was the best within our nation.
When we'd done wrong punishment we
  got.
When Dad swung strap she cried a lot.
She ran Postoffice, for resort cooked meals,
She knit our sox and darned our heels.
Played organ in church, taught piano to
  kids.
Put food in jars and turned the lids.
Her lot was hard, her work a strain.
There was always smile, no word of
  complain.
As years roll by, more plainly I see,
God made only one, and that was she.

Minnesota Winter

Out window we see mercury down does
  creep,
While snow piles up in drifts so deep.
We like the cold, we like the snow,
Doesn't matter to us, let the north winds
  blow.
Carry in the wood, some kindling too,
Night without a fireplace would surely
  never do.
Light pipe and fire, we're in for fun.
Time takes on flight like a shot from a gun.
There are snacks galore, we pop the corn.
Who wants to retire till early morn?
We do not envy those lying on sand.
When summer comes here, t'will seem
  more grand.
There's feeling of regret when evenings are
  thru.
They're all too short, Minnesota winters are
  too.

An early Bay Lake baseball team - third from left on top, Alec.
Sitting L to R: Ed, Max, and fourth from left, Bill.

On the Farm in the Early Century

The clock showed four, our school let out,
All rushed for door with many a shout.
To woods we ran with no slow pace,
Joy time was short as we all knew.
Nighttime was falling, much work to do
Wood must be bucked, hungry stove be fed,
So later to enjoy its roaring red.
To barn we go, all painted bright red—
Horses, cows, and pigs all must be fed.
Haymow we climb and pitch down hay,
And think of sweat on putting-up day.
We start to milk, the cats say meow,
We hit their mouths direct from cow.
Our chores all done, to home we go.
Again our speed is not so slow.
Supper's over, mittens and socks on wire,
The time of day we never do tire.
The women knit socks or finish a seam,
Our Dad he reads Arpeliar Reason.
We study some lessons, over history we pore.
We're glad there never will be more war.
From time to time the lamps go low.
Get up to pump, to make them glow.
Go to bed, no use to gripe,
Early in the morning he raps stovepipe.
We get up quick, no second thump,
Or up he comes two steps a jump.
For you who have never laid on hay,
Or heard cows chew, or horses neigh,
Weaned a calf or milked a cow,
You've missed a lot, that's all for now!

It was stated in an article printed in the <u>St. Paul Pioneer Press</u> dated August 31, 1941, that Alec had wanted to be a lawyer and Max, an accountant. Ed and Bill, both with mechanical leanings, were interested in automobiles.

Chapter Three

The Story of Alexander and Myrle and their Influence on Ruttger's Growth

Alec Ruttger's graduation photo.

Alexander John, or Alec, as he was known, attended high school in Brainerd after he had completed the eighth grade in the rural Bay Lake school. He attended school in Brainerd for two years, then completed his high school education and graduated from Central High School in Duluth with the class of 1912. All four years of high school he boarded out, working for room and board. He said he began to help take care of resort guest fishermen when he was seven. He caught minnows and frogs, cleaned fish, bailed boats, and I am sure, worked in the gardens. When he was old enough, Alec went to North Dakota where he worked on threshing machines to make

Alec in World War I uniform which he wore to his last Memorial Day parade in 1977 without alterations.

extra money for the family. Alec was inducted into the Army on February 2, 1918, went into the 20th Engineers, and was sent to France on March 29, 1918. He was listed as being a chauffeur. He spent 14 months in the foot of the Alps, while serving in World War I. He was let out of the service at Camp Dodge, Iowa, on June 9, 1919. After getting out of the Army, Alec went to Helena, Montana, to homestead property, but soon decided that was not for him. He told me that it was too remote and that whenever the wind stopped blowing you looked out to see what was wrong. He returned to Bay Lake.

With youth and a great deal of vigor, Alec did what many said could not be done. He developed a first class resort in the wilds of northern Minnesota. An ad appeared in the <u>Deerwood Enterprise</u> dated June 25, 1920, saying "The Bay Lake Summer Resort is open and prepared to accommodate you with boats, cabins, and board. Good fishing, etc. Make this your summer home. Phone or write A. J. Ruttger, Deerwood, Minn." The resort accommodated 40 people at that time.

He borrowed $3,500 from a bank when he first

The Bay Lake Summer Resort is 5½ miles south of Deerwood, Minnesota, in Crow Wing County 108 miles from Duluth, 126 miles from Minneapolis, on best of roads, rain or shine—just an evening's spin after a week-end visit with the family at the lake. ¶Good bass, pike and other fishing. Car shed for your car, boating, evinruding, bathing, tennis, croquet, quoits. Modern store in which to buy your fishing tackle. ¶ The Bay Lake Summer Resort is situated on the banks of Bay Lake the beautiful, with forty miles of shore line, cut up by many bays, points, isthmuses and islands. In close proximity to other beautiful lakes, bountiful with fish. ¶ Meals are first-class—home cooking. Apartments consist of cabins, sleeping porches, bath room.

1920 advertisement. Note the $3 rate per day for lodging, three meals, and a boat. You got hot water too!

ON SCENIC HIGHWAY, BLACK DIAMOND AND GREEN & WHITE TRAILS

The Bay Lake Summer Resort

P. O. Deerwood, Minnesota.

A. J. Ruttger, Manager

IN THE HEART OF THE TEN THOUSAND LAKES REGION

Write for Reservations
Trains met by request.

Rates for Room and Board:
$21 to $23 per week.

ENTRANCE TO RUTTGER'S BAY LAKE LODGE DEERWOOD, MINN. B-3175

Birch entrance sign at Ruttger's - early 1930s.

View on arrival at Ruttger's Bay Lake Lodge.

took over the business in order to make improvements he felt were needed. At that time there was only a small dining room, a part of the house, and an overflow with tables set in a screened-in porch on the east side of the house. All tablecloths were clipped on to the tables to keep the wind from blowing them off. In 1922, Alec decided a new dining hall was needed, and he built a log building separate from the lodge-house building, to the west, where it

is located at this time.

Alec married Minnie Marsh on May 23, 1920. She was born December 6, 1894, in Hutchinson, graduated from Aitkin High School, then went on to teach. Minnie died in September of 1923 of a diabetic coma. Minnie must have worked in the business as I found records in the resort attic that had her signature on them. She also must have played piano as there was sheet music in the attic that has her name,

Ruttger's new dining hall - 1922.

Myrle's baby picture.

according to their location. Children generally had to walk to and from school. People brought up in that era tell of walking to and from school in the dark during the winter season and hearing wolves howling. The roads were dirt so in the spring they sometimes became impassable to wagons and then automobiles and very difficult to walk on also. As you see, life was not easy for people raised in those days—no jumping into a car and driving to Brainerd for a hamburger. Going to town was a big event and had to be planned for to allow enough time to travel by daylight. My earliest memories do include automobiles—the kind with tires that needed patching every so often. So, I'm not sure when people started using automobiles instead of the horse-drawn vehicles. Anyway, that was when Myrle and Alec grew up, in the days of traveling by horse-drawn buggies, wagons, and sleighs. Alec lived near the school,

as well as some with Josephine's name.

Alec married Myrle Fuller on September 14, 1924, in Princeton, Minnesota. Myrle Margaret Fuller was born in Marshall, Minnesota, to Frank and Elizabeth Skillings Fuller on September 11, 1901. Myrle finished school and went on to Normal Training to become a teacher. She taught in country schools at Esden and Dagget Brook. Myrle grew up in the Bay Lake area about a mile and a half from the Ruttger property. She was one of seven children: Myrle, Mable, Asa, Mason, Ethel, Edith, and Davis; Ethel died at an early age. Myrle was raised on a small berry farm where they all worked very hard to make a living. She remembered wearing stockings on her arms to keep from being scratched by berry bushes.

Myrle attended grade school at the Bay Lake schoolhouse as did the children in that certain area. There were a number of small country schools in those days so the children went where they were ordered

Myrle Ruttger.

but Myrle had to walk quite a distance. Then after she finished her education she taught in country schools where the teacher was expected to start the fire for heat in the morning, as well as see that the place was clean and ready for students—indoors and outdoors. Since the school was a distance from where her family lived, she stayed with residents of the area where she was teaching.

Alec and Myrle lived in a house built by the Young family, just to the west of the home of Joe and Josie. They worked hard to make a go of the resort. Myrle took care of the family, as well as

Alec and Myrle's wedding photo.

Muddy road on the way to Deerwood.

doing secretarial work in her home in the winter and at the lodge in the summer. She also answered reservation calls in the home, as well as at the resort in the earlier days. In addition, she was in charge of keeping many of the flower gardens in order—planting and weeding. Of course, there were not nearly the number of plants that there are today. Myrle was a rather quiet person, in contrast to Alec who had to be on the go and out with people. Myrle had some very bad medical problems in 1964. She had diverticulitis while in Florida in the winter and was saved only because they had the new miracle drugs to work with. In February of 1978, she had a recurrence while living at Bay Lake and died in the hospital on February 5, 1978. She was buried on February 7th in the Bay Lake Cemetery.

Alec and Myrle's golden anniversary, 1974.

Scene on the road near Bay Lake, Minn.

THE PEOPLE WE MET

A humorous postcard that used early "trick photography."

RUTTGER LODGE ON BAY LAKE.
Deerwood, Minnesota. Telephone and railway
connections. 124 miles north from Minneapolis.
Take Trail No. 3 to Elk River, thence Big 4 Lakes
Trail to our doors.
Beautiful lakes and woods.

POST CARD

Miss Jerry Fenstenmacher,
Chapman,
Kansas.

The Family of Alexander and Myrle

Alec and Myrle were blessed with three children: Mae Elizabeth, Alexander John Jr. (Jack), and Jane Anne. As stated before, Myrle did correspondence for Alec year-round and also worked in the business all through the years—mainly in the office, besides taking care of their home and raising three offspring. Following are some of our statistics:

I, **Mae Elizabeth**, was born on September 14, 1926, at the old Miner's Hospital in Crosby. I started school in Deerwood, the first year the Bay Lake School was not in operation. We were the first students from Bay Lake to go to school by bus. At the resort, I guided horseback rides on trails, did secretarial work and mailings, front desk, reservations, baking, salad department work, head bookkeeper from 1970 until computers were installed, and am doing payroll to date. I graduated from high school in Crosby-Ironton and attended one year of junior college there also. I then

Jack, Mae, Jane, and Alec.

graduated from Grinnell College in Grinnell, Iowa, the spring of 1948, with a major in Business and Economics. John Arnold Heglund and I were married on September 29, 1956. We had two children—Eric John and Laura Jane. Eric is married to Teresa Blakesley, and they live in Ironton. They have two sons: Adam and Alex. Eric worked at the resort on the beach (rented boats and motors and did clean-up), worked in the Golf Pro Shop, did some dining room busing, inventory on computers, and night audit for a time. Laura worked on the playground, in the gift and clothing shops, bookkeeping a couple of summers, and front desk. She is working in Minneapolis at this time. Arnold, as we called him, died on November 24, 1990.

Alexander John Jr. (Jack), was born in Crosby on December 19, 1929. He attended Crosby-Ironton schools and graduated in 1948. He attended the University of Minnesota but did not graduate because he was inducted into the Army—where he became a cook. He and Ann Hanlon were married on May 23, 1953, while Jack was in the Army. Their son, Alexander John III (better known as Sandy) was born in the Army camp at Fort Leonard Wood. After

Jack, Myrle, Jane, and Mae.

Jack was discharged from the Army, they had the rest of their family: Julia Ann, Christopher Joseph, and Mary Catherine. Sadly, Sandy was killed in an accident in November of 1973 while attending school in Florida. Julie married Perry Platisha, and they have four children—Molly, Blake, Jordan, and Casey. Mary married Tom Witchger, and they live in Plymouth, Minnesota. Chris is not married at this time. Jack's family worked in different capacities at the resort as described in the story of their family.

Jane Anne was born on August 29, 1934, also in Crosby. She attended school in Crosby-Ironton, and graduated in 1952. Jane worked at the resort on the children's playground, dining room, and front desk. She attended Hamline University for a year, and then fell in love and was married to Peter Bobich. They had four children:

Deborah Anne, Frederick Mark, Pamela Mae, and Todd Michael. Debbie worked on the playground, dining room, front desk, and appeared in ski shows. She married Randy Erickson and they have two children: Ryan and Janelle. Fred worked at the resort on the beach, in the dining room, skied in ski shows, was head of sales for a time, and was general manager from 1990 to 1992. He married Gwynne Kangas, and they are parents of Joshua, Steffani, and Abbi. Fred and family are living near Grand Rapids and manage Ruttger's Sugar Lake Lodge. Pam worked at the resort on the playground, dining room, front desk, and appeared in ski shows. She is married to Marlan Caillier. They have two daughters: Annie and Alison. They live in the Monticello area. Todd worked in the dining room, bar, and golf course. He is not yet married and lives in the Crosby area.

Jane, Jack, Alec, and Mae.

Front of main lodge, about 1930, overlooking Bay Lake before bar area was added.

Historical Records During Alec's Period of Operations

Alec said that during the depression in 1932 business was so slow that Ruttger's was down to four guests in the first week of August. Forced to discharge all their help because they were not able to pay them, the family did most of the work themselves, sometimes aided by the guests. Alec and Max went to Florida in October of 1933 and stayed for a month in St. Petersburg. They visited there to investigate new methods of publicizing in order to get tourists to visit northern Minnesota.

An article in the Brainerd Dispatch dated November 27, 1933, said the resort had been in operation for 40 years at that time. The same article said it was anticipated that increased business would occur at Bay Lake and at Brainerd due to improvement of state trunk highway number 18.

Alec was active in many organizations.

He helped organize and was the first president of the Minnesota Resort Association. Approximately 35 Minnesota resort owners met in Brainerd at the Ransford Hotel on Saturday, February 4, 1943, to organize the association which was formed to resolve problems confronting state resorts in the coming summer. They had to contend with a shortage of labor, food rationing, and other restrictions due to the war. He lobbied many times for the state's industry at the Minnesota legislature and stomped the state preaching the value of tourism to its economy. It was his idea to put "Land of 10,000 Lakes" on Minnesota's license plates, and it still appears there today. When he took over management of the resort, Alec borrowed money and built 12 small cabins on the lakeshore. He also enlarged the lodge (Ruttger home) building

Ruttger's nine-hole golf course. Note the cattle in the background.

Diving platform.

Water wheel.

and added a large kitchen. He and his family moved into tents so they could rent their own living quarters during the season. Ruttger's was among the first to advertise private baths and hot running water (fueled by coal) in each dwelling. He started a golf course in 1921, where fences kept cows off the sand greens.

In the <u>American Resort</u> magazine dated July 1929, there was a write-up about Ruttger's Resort. It said there was a large log building which served as a dining hall and lounge. There were 24 cabins, a general store, a garage, a sporty nine-hole golf course, a baseball diamond, a tennis court, and a trap-shooting court. Most cabins consisted of one, two, and three rooms. Those on the lake had private baths, circulating hot water, heat radiation, and cobblestone

GOLF LINKS

fireplaces. They contained sleeping quarters only. There were only two or three housekeeping cabins located quite a distance from the dining hall. There was quite a lot of electrical equipment in the lodge kitchen—peelers, mixers, dishwasher, automatic egg boiler, toasters, electric refrigerator, power ice cream and sherbet freezer, and an ice cube and dessert cabinet.

Alec cleaning the beach.
If it needed to be done, he did it.

Water sports equipment was available—toboggans, water wheel, diving raft with spring boards, swings, trapeze, a cedar log anchored with

swivel chain for rolling contests, and on the beach were bath houses and lockers. Along the lakeshore was a dancing and bathing pavilion, known as the "Green Lantern." There were dances in the summer every Tuesday, Thursday, and Saturday put on by an excellent orchestra. The same orchestra played every weekday evening and on Sunday noon during dinners in the log dining hall. The University of Minnesota orchestra had played the past several years.

CABIN 25 AT RUTTGER'S BAY LAKE LODGE DEERWOOD, MINN.

Old number 16— the Ruttger family lived here during the fall of 1940 when their new house was being built. Mae, Jack, and Jane spent the night alone on November 11th during the famous Armistice Day blizzard when "Mom and Dad" could not get home from their Armistice Day banquet in Crosby.

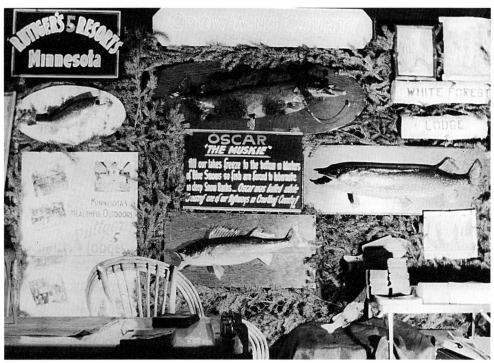

The sport show booth—1940—featuring Oscar, "The Muskie."

There were seven saddle horses and ponies available for riding. A hostess was engaged for evening entertainment. Her duty was also to inspect cabins and dining rooms to see that they were in order. The resort had just purchased a 32 horsepower outboard motor to be placed on a speedboat. The motor weighed 110 pounds and could also be used on a larger passenger boat.

Alec had boundless energy, and decided that winters were too long, so he operated a resort called Pirates Cove located on the Florida Keys during the winter of 1935 - 1936. He and his brother, Max, leased the property from a widow, with the idea of possibly purchasing. I remember my family traveled by car, and upon arrival at Miami found that there had been a hurricane which had wiped out the bridge connecting the mainland with the Keys. We had to wait for a week to catch the ferry that traveled to the Keys. When we arrived at the resort there were many insects and snakes that had been left by the hurricane. We stayed in Key West until the property could be made safer. Jack and I attended school that winter in a country school on Big Pine Key which we reached by riding on a bus. Dad only operated the resort for one winter, so I guess he did not feel it was very profitable.

Alec worked the Bay Lake property from when he took it over in 1920 until his

Jane, Jack, and Mae at Pirate's Cove.

death in May of 1978 at the age of 85. Ruttger's Bay Lake Lodge back in the 1920s, 1930s, 1940s, 1950s, and 1960s operated basically from Memorial Day to Labor Day. In the 1960s, it was decided to try group sales meetings, and efforts were made to attract business before Memorial Day and after Labor Day. Alec passed away at his home on Sunday, May 7, 1978. He was buried in the Bay Lake Cemetery on May 10th. ✺

School bus in the Florida Keys. The school was on Big Pine. The teacher, Sue Moore; the year, 1935. Today, the school in Marathon on the Keys is named the Sue Moore Elementary School.

Newspaper Articles from 1933

Brainerd Resort Operator Gives Ideas Gleaned on Florida Visit

A. J. Ruttger, of Ruttger's Bay Lake Lodge, Deerwood, Minnesota, has returned from a month's stay in St. Petersburg, Florida. The Bay Lake lodge has been in operation 40 years, and during that period has been an extensive advertiser using all possible means of publicity. His visit to Florida was to investigate any new methods of publicity.

Mr. Ruttger, during his stay, investigated all angles of Florida promotion work and business expected for the coming winter tourist season. Florida expects a better tourist season than last year, said Mr. Ruttger. Rates are quite reasonable in hotel and apartment houses. A marked increase of Illinois cars was noticed in Florida.

Every hotel and apartment house endeavors to have its guests register at the Chamber of Commerce. So heavy is the registration, that books in St. Petersburg Chamber of Commerce are listed according to the different states. This makes a permanent record and is used for publicity work. It makes it interesting to the visitors, for they can scan their state book and see what friends or neighbors have arrived and where to find them. The newspapers run these records, columns daily by states, indicating the new arrivals. Many a tourist buys a St. Petersburg paper and sends it home because his name was mentioned and in turn may induce somebody else to visit Florida.

A plan like this is now under consideration by the Brainerd Chamber of Commerce. The registrations would give the tourist's name, home address, and lake address and would be especially useful in locating him for inquiries by telephone, Western Union, etc. The list would also be used in sending out lake literature and other publicity.

Mr. Ruttger considers the Century of Progress at Chicago to have been a success the first year, but so far as repeating it in 1934, the fair is a "has been." No visitor will repeat, he said. It was good for one year because the whole country supported it. But next year will find all legitimate natural resort business striving to regain business lost to the fair in 1933.

Mr. Ruttger had been named a member of the Brainerd Chamber of Commerce Tourist and Advertising committee, a reappointment, for President D. C. Gray is aware of the years of experience Mr.

Early morning fishing got these Chicagoans their limit of six bass a piece in less than two hours at Ruttger's Bay Lake Lodge near Deerwood, Minnesota. Shown with their catch are Mrs. H.W. Stone; Ted Bateman, guide; W.C. Dyer; H. W. Stone; and Larry Wolfe. Holding the lower string of bass are Gil Lyman, guide, and Miss Gertrude Dyer.

Ruttger has had in advertising and other publicity. Ruttgers, Inc. now conducts the Bay Lake lodge near Deerwood and the Pine Beach lodge.

Courier Candids...
(March 21, 1956)
Alec Ruttger
Service in Many Fields

The name of Ruttger has become synonymous in many parts of the country with the pleasant word, vacation. People in Kansas and in Florida, as well as in other parts of the country, go with one accord to

Conservation leaders and resort owners joined with the water and hunting section of Minnesota safety council in a luncheon Friday at the Curtis Hotel, in connection with Northwest Sportsman's show. Shown front row, seated, left to right, are Alec Ruttger, president, Minnesota Resort Association; A. V. Rohweder, safety council president; Len Brisley, chairman, water and hunting section; and standing, C. L. Wilson, conservation commissioner. Back row, standing, left to right; E. V. Willard, deputy conservation commissioner; Val Saxby, secretary of Arrowhead Association; A.E. Searls, secretary, water and hunting section of safety council; and C. B. Zealand, safety council executive secretary.

Ruttger's when they want pleasure-packed, sun-filled vacation days.

The "Ruttger story" is not one of overnight success. . . it is a recountable saga of a man, Joseph Ruttger, and his four sons: Alec, Bill, Ed, and Max. It is a story of a family that came here in 1886, a family that will without a question continue to prosper and bring commendable notice to the areas in which they live and work.

The elder Joseph Ruttger came to the Bay Lake area in 1886 and homesteaded on the small island. Two years later, he moved to the mainland and built on the site of the present Ruttger Resort, now ably run by his son, Alec Ruttger.

It would be difficult to set a date on the official beginning of Ruttger's Bay Lake resort. In early days fishermen were brought by team to the Ruttger home where they were outfitted with boats and bait, were fed at the family table, and later bedded down in the haymow. When they left, they paid what they felt the service had been worth.

There were four resorts, as such, in the Bay Lake area in those early days – Youngs, Archibalds, Soules, and Ruttger's. Guests partook of the harvests from the gardens and huge berry plots, of the meat that was butchered and cured at annual butchering, of the milk, cheeses, eggs, etc., from the "home-owned" cows and chickens. Guests in early resort days were members of the family!

It was in this environment that Alec Ruttger and his brothers were raised. Trained to help both in the farming chores and in the entertaining of guests, the Ruttger boys came to have wide experience and new and progressive ideas in resorting.

Alec attended school at Brainerd and Duluth before going off to World War I. He

Alec and his wife in the dining room with guests.

spent 14 months in the foothills of the Alps, serving with the 20th Engineers. Shortly after his return, he bought out the growing resort business from his father and set out on a new type of venture.

The "fishermen's house," a large dormitory-like building was changed over into a place for the summer employees to live. Alec Ruttger built 12 small cottages on the lake shore for guests to stay; he and his family moving into tents themselves so that they might rent out every available space to guests. The Ruttger cabins at Bay Lake were among the very first to be able to advertise private baths with hot water heaters (fueled by coal) in each dwelling.

Ruttger's Bay Lake Lodge now has 36 cottages, all gas heated, each walled in knotty pine, and having picture windows. Ultramodern guest rooms with wall-to-wall carpeting, colored bath fixtures, and other luxuries are provided in the main building. The dining room accommodates upward of 140 guests. There are facilities for entertaining large conventions and groups as well as families and honeymooning couples.

Alec Ruttger has worked hard and continues to do so, spurred on by the pride in his site on the lake as well as the vacation calling area in which he lives. Active in a number of resort and vacationland groups, Alec has served as president of both the Minnesota Resort Association and the Paul Bunyan Vacationland group.

He has also served well as commander of the VFW post, as a lay-leader in the Methodist church, and for a number of years as chairman of the Republican party in Crow Wing county.

Alec Ruttger is blessed with a combination of qualities, a love of the out-of-doors, and a genuine interest in his fellowman. These things have brought him a successful life, not only in the business he has built but in the number of friends, as well. His philosophy is one indeed to be emulated and admired exceedingly.

Resort Owners Association Is Formed At Meeting

Approximately 35 Minnesota Resort owners convened at Brainerd on February 2, 1943, to organize a Minnesota Resort Owners Association and elect temporary officers. The meeting was held at Ransford Hotel.

The association outlined at the meeting included promotional and advertising of Minnesota resorts and the education of members in promoting and holding the good will of tourist guests.

First Annual Meeting
Minnesota Resort Association

Nicollet Hotel - Dec. 16-17, '43

From Crosby Courier dated 2/8/43

Permanent officers are to be elected at a meeting of the association to be held in Brainerd March 7.

Alec Ruttger, Bay Lake, was elected temporary president of the association and R. E. Richeson, secretary of the Crow Wing County Tourist Boosters' Association, was named temporary secretary.

A committee to prepare a list of candidates for permanent office and outline a program for the association was named Saturday including: Alec Ruttger, Bay Lake; J. W. Seely, Garrison; A.C. Anderson, Tower; F. R. McGregor, Aitkin; Max J. Ruttger, Brainerd; Merill Cragun, Brainerd; Tom Villelli, Deerwood; and R. E. Richeson.

H. A. Bray, representing the ODT, was a guest of the resort owners and outlined the schedule of bus and truck reaction plans relative to summer transportation plans.

Victor Johnston, secretary of the Minnesota Tourist Bureau, Minneapolis, and Vern Turnquist, St. Paul Pioneer Press, were guests of the resort owners.

THE MINNESOTA RESORT ASSN.

is pleased to announce that the following of its members will be open this summer:

Resort	Location
Shingwauk Resort	Aitkin
Geneva Beach Hotel	Alexandria
Beecher's Resort	Annandale
Joe's Lodge	Bemidji
Ruttger's Birchmont Lodge	Bemidji
Wolf Lake Resort	Bemidji
Bittner's Resort	Bovey
Cragun's on Pine Beach	Brainerd
Grandview Lodge	Brainerd
Island View Lodge	Brainerd
Madden's Pine Beach Lodge	Brainerd
Pine Beach Golf Course	Brainerd
Robert's Pine Beach Hotel	Brainerd
Ruttger's Pine Beach Lodge	Brainerd
Sunset Point Resort	Cohasset
Chap's Lodge	Cook
Pehrson's Lodge	Cook
Nelson's Crane Lake Cabins	Crane Lake
Bonnie Lakes Farm	Cross Lake
Ruttger's Bay Lake Lodge	Deerwood
Fair Hills Resort	Detroit Lakes
Mari-Mac Court	Detroit Lakes
Hibbard's Lodge	Ely
Blue Goose Resort	Garrison
Peter's Sunset Beach Hotel	Glenwood
Pokegama Hotel	Grand Rapids
"The Androy" Hotel	Hibbing
Squaw Point Resort	Hillman
Camp Idlewild	Marcel
Idlewilde Resort	Osakis
Birchdale Villas	Pequot Lakes
Ruttger's Shady Point Lodge	Pequot Lakes
Platwood Country Club	Platwood
Anderson's Birch Point Inn	Tower
Steege's Bayview Inn	Tower
Vermillion Beach Resort	Tower
Chase Resort Hotel	Walker
Forestview Lodge	Walker
Journey's End Lodge	Walker
Miller's Cedar Springs Lodge	Walker

For full particulars write any of the above listed member resorts.

Chapter Four
Jack and Ann's Story

Alexander John (Jack) Ruttger Jr. was born December 19, 1929, in Crosby. Jack always enjoyed sports, and usually had a team of locals to play basketball on the tennis courts, as well as baseball and football on the lawns. He was very good at water-skiing, as well as winter snow skiing. He graduated from Crosby-Ironton schools in 1948 and attended the University of Minnesota. He was inducted into the Army before he finished college. He served as a cook for officers in the Army, so he gained experience and knowledge of quantity cooking.

Jack and Ann Hanlon were married May 23, 1953, while Jack was in the Army. Together they operated Ruttger's Key Colony Beach Motel in Marathon Key, Florida, for a number of years and were in charge of operating

Jack and Ann at Fort Riley, Kansas.

Ruttger's Bay Lake Lodge from 1955 until their son, Christopher, took over management in 1992. They still participate in operations, though not directly the general managers any longer. Jack is president of Ruttger's Bay Lake Lodge. He has been very active in many organizations: Minnesota Hotel Association (president in 1977), Minnesota Resort Association (president in 1971), and Minnesota Resorter of the Year in 1981, president of the Brainerd Chamber of Commerce, St. Joseph's Hospital Board (chairman from 1990-1993), and has been very active in the

Brainerd Rotary Club (past president). Jack was Brainerd Citizen of the Year in 1986. Jack is also a member of the Resort Committee of the American Hotel and Motel Association and was its chairman in 1989. In 1991, Jack was appointed by Congressman James Oberstar to serve on the House Tourism Caucus Advisory Board in Washington, D.C. which he chaired in 1993-1994. He was appointed to be a delegate to the first White House Conference on Tourism in November 1995. In 1994, Jack received an award for the "Outstanding Individual in Tourism" at the annual Minnesota Tourism Conference.

Ann has been a prominent part of the resort. In the early days, she was Jack's secretary and could do anything he did, except the sewer work. Truly, the resort could not have operated without her.

In the evenings, Ann and Susie Kolliner from Stillwater, Minnesota, (pictured on page 62) would entertain guests by playing organ and piano duets night after night, and the guests loved it!

Besides her job as back-up to Jack and "professional" entertainer, she oversaw the stores, the Gift Shop and the Country Store, as she does to this day.

Ann was a stay-at-home mother, who raised four children, did all of the above, and put up with a husband who put in many long hours.

Ann and Jack's wedding picture.

The Family of Jack and Ann

Ann and Jack's family consisted of four children. Alexander John III (Sandy) was the oldest. In November of 1973, he was killed in an automobile accident in south Miami, Florida. Sandy was attending Miami Dade Community College on a tennis scholarship, with the full intent of continuing his education at Florida International University, majoring in Hotel Management.

The next oldest is Julia Ruttger Platisha.

Blake, JP, and Molly Platisha, 1986, Julie Ruttger Platisha's children.

Tom and Mary Witchger with mascot Rudi at 1996 Oktoberfest celebration.

Julie is married and lives in the Brainerd area with her husband, Perry, and family-- Molly, Blake, JP, and Casey. Julie worked during her school years at the resort in the gift shop and the dining room. She graduated from Rollins College in Winter Park, Florida, after attending St. Catherine's in St. Paul for three years.

Mary Ruttger Witchger and her husband, Tom, live in the Minneapolis area. They were married on April 29, 1995. Mary was very active around the resort, having worked in the gift shops, dining room, and Kids' Kamp. She graduated from St. Thomas College in St. Paul. She also worked for three years at Walt Disney World in their resorts.

Christopher has a section in this book, though it does not touch on his background. Chris worked at almost every job there was at the resort to really learn the trade well. During his college years, he worked one summer at Grand Hotel on Mackinac Island in Michigan. He graduat-

ed from Cornell University in Ithaca, New York, with a degree in Hotel Management.

During their teen-age years, Sandy and Julie were involved in many ski shows which were held every Saturday afternoon. Julie swam in the synchronized swim acts and Sandy skied barefoot and went over the ski jump along with his cousin, Fred, and many other employees who loved to ski. Those were great times and are remembered by so many! The seven-person pyramids were spectacular with Julie and the waitresses standing on the shoulders of Sandy, Fred, and the boys. Oh for the good old days.

Jack, Sandy, and Ann.

Lloyd Kolliner, Stillwater, Howard and Jeanne Van, St. Paul, Susie Kolliner, long-time guests and friends.

Todd Bobich (6) and Chris Ruttger (4) at Ruttger's stable.

Chapter Five
The Ruttger Family's History as Resort Operators

There was a period in time when there were five Ruttger resorts—each one separately owned and operated. Ruttger's Bay Lake Lodge was started in about 1898. Ruttger's Pine Beach Lodge on Gull Lake was built and operated by Max and his sons, Buzz and Don, beginning in 1930. It was leased to Madden's Resort in 1969 and later sold to Madden's. It is known as Madden's Pine Portage at this time and is used exclusively for group housing. Bill built Ruttger's Shady Point Lodge on Whitefish Lake in 1936, with the official opening date of July 4th. It was in operation until 1979 when it was sold. Shady Point property had been purchased in 1934 at a price of $1,200. Bill's son, Joe, told us that when he and Carol took over operation of Shady Point in 1958 there were 18 persons registered to vote in Ideal Township where they were located, and by 1979 there were 1,003. Ed operated Ruttger's Sherwood Forest, located between Gull and Margaret Lakes, from 1935 until 1946, at which time he sold and went out of the business. Don, Max's son, has operated Ruttger's Birchmont Lodge near Bemidji since 1937, and his son, Randy, has now taken over. The only two of the original resorts still in business at this time are Ruttger's Bay Lake Lodge and Ruttger's Birchmont. In addition, for some time, there were Ruttger motels in Florida. Max, Don, and Buzz built a motel at Lauderdale-by-the-Sea and operated it for a number of years. They also built another motel at Fort Lauderdale which they operated for a short time. These have both been sold. Alec and

Cousin Joe and Jack in the speedboat, 1935.

Alec and his advertising car. Notice "Ruttger's 5 Better Resorts." He would never say "best" as that would be boasting.

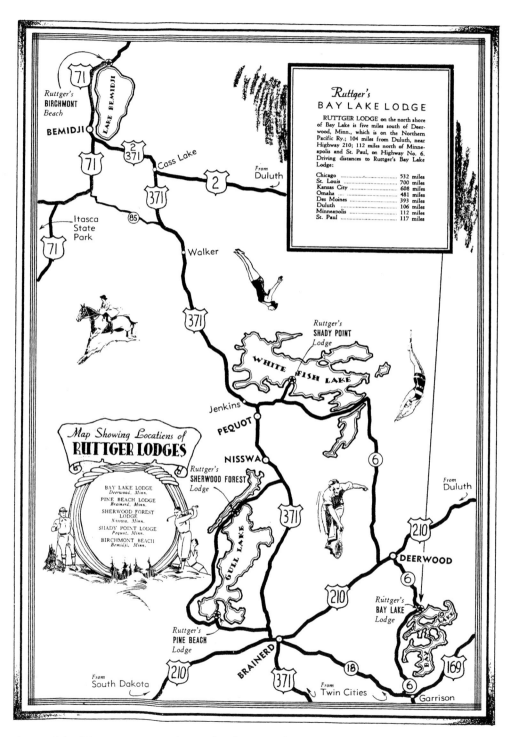

Ruttger's
BAY LAKE LODGE

RUTTGER LODGE on the north shore of Bay Lake is five miles south of Deerwood, Minn., which is on the Northern Pacific Ry.; 104 miles from Duluth, near Highway 210; 112 miles north of Minneapolis and St. Paul, on Highway No. 6. Driving distances to Ruttger's Bay Lake Lodge:

Chicago	532 miles
St. Louis	700 miles
Kansas City	608 miles
Omaha	481 miles
Des Moines	393 miles
Duluth	106 miles
Minneapolis	112 miles
St. Paul	117 miles

Map Showing Locations of
RUTTGER LODGES

BAY LAKE LODGE
Deerwood, Minn.
PINE BEACH LODGE
Brainerd, Minn.
SHERWOOD FOREST LODGE
Nisswa, Minn.
SHADY POINT LODGE
Pequot, Minn.
BIRCHMONT BEACH
Bemidji, Minn.

A map of the 5 Ruttger Resorts, each owned and operated by a Ruttger.

A popular ad used by five Ruttger Resorts in the 1930s.

Jack owned and operated a motel at Marathon, in the Florida Keys, for a number of years, but this has also been sold. Ruttger's Sugar Lake Lodge, Grand Rapids, Minnesota, is a very new operation. Fred Bobich (son of Jane Ruttger Bobich) and his wife, Gwynne, became the owners and operators in 1993. They live on the property with their children. They built a lodge building, an 18-hole golf course, and refurbished the restaurant now known as "Jack's." They also remodeled cabins and condominiums on the property and have recently added condominiums attached to the lodge building which greatly add to their lodging capacity.

The Sands Motel in Marathon, Florida Keys, 1957.

Duncan Hines, hotel and restaurant critic, Jack Ruttger, Alec Ruttger, and Mr. Coates of Coates Hotel in Virginia, Minnesota, during a visit to Ruttger's Keys Motor Lodge in 1958.

Bay Lake Summer Resort. Note the road was where the pool is now. The name before Ruttger's Bay Lake Lodge was Bay Lake Summer Resort (sign on the tree).

Joseph and Josephine as Tourist Hosts

Joseph and Josephine were the first of the Ruttger family in the resort business—though that was not their original intent. They were hospitable, served good food, and they furnished good accommodations for their guests. Of course, the original attraction was something that is still true today and something you cannot change --- Location! Location! Location! Accessibility to the property, the outstanding view from the small hill overlooking the lake, the north-shore location, and the fact that there was enough land available so that they were not penned in, all made for a good spot to set up a resort. When Joe and Josie operated the resort, it was known as The Bay Lake Summer Resort. (There are registration books with that name at the top.)

The whole family worked to keep the place going in the early days, much like the early farms. (I have heard that farmers had large families, as they were useful in doing work on their farms.) So much had to be done by hand. The boys seined minnows for bait and took people fishing, but were not allowed to charge unless somebody wanted to tip them.

They lived in the building that had been set up by the Pioneer Cooperative Company as a company store. The company had disbanded after about a year, and the store building was left vacant. Bill Ruttger said the last three sons born to Joseph and Josephine were born in that building. Bill, the youngest, was born in 1899, and I would guess that they would have built

Sign on Highway 18, five miles from the resort– 1920. This tells it all. "Always a crowd of young folks." Note the old men!

their large white house in about 1901.

At first there was no charge, just a sociability to help people that had come a distance and had no place to stay. Then, as time went by, a chance was seen to start making some income by charging for shelter and food. I am sure this must have been an aid in providing a living for people in the area as the land is not particularly suited to farming.

In the early days, the resort was manned by the family, and later as the need arose people from the area were paid for helping. At first there were no bathroom facilities indoors as that was before the time of such conveniences. Then, as time went by, running water was piped in and each unit had its own hot water heater. The only phone, in the house of Joe and Josie, had a crank used for the number of rings listed for the number to be called. Long distance calls had to go through an operator sitting at a switchboard in Deerwood. Food was grown and butchered by the family except for the fish that were caught. Most of the people that came were met at the railroad depot in Deerwood, as roads were not in very good condition.

Grandma Josephine did the cooking. They had about five or six girls that did the

Ruttger workers.

serving of food in the early days, probably with other duties as well. At that time the yards and gardens were cleaned up and tended by members of the Ruttger family themselves. Of course, there was the "mowing" of the fairways on the golf course by the horses and cows.

Alec and Myrle as Resort Operators

Alec took over the operation of Ruttger's Resort in 1920. He immediately made major changes and improvements. He borrowed $3,500 from a bank to build 12 cottages and remodel the entire property. Many years he borrowed money in the spring in order to improve and enlarge, then worked very hard to make the payments. He had a log dining room built in 1922 and sent out invitations to its

Ruttger's Bay Lake Lodge in the 1930s. Grandpa Joe and friend. Note the old house with the porch.

grand opening: "Yourself and intimate friends are cordially invited to attend the opening of Ruttger's large new log dining hall at Bay Lake, on Tuesday, June twentieth, with a Chicken Dinner at 6:00 p.m., and a Dance afterwards." In 1921, Mr. Haas "Zig" Ziegler was instrumental in building a nine-hole golf course at Ruttger's Bay Lake, with the fairways mowed by cows and horses. The Green Lantern dance hall, built in 1925, was a popular meeting place for many years. Alec had finished paying his parents for the resort in 1931 in spite of the fact that the country was in a depression. In a letter sent out to Bay Lake and Gull Lake prospects, the spring of 1933, it was stated that both places had new log lounge rooms, home-cooked meals, boats, concrete tennis courts, golf with grass greens, and children's playground instructors. In a letter the spring of 1934, it stated that the Bay Lake location had covered the entire waterfront with 700 cubic yards of sand. All of the main lodge was covered with varnished logs, as well as being connected to the dining room. Up until that time, the Ruttger home had still been white, but now was covered with logs. During the depression times, the latter 1930s, Alec tried another attempt to interest more people in coming to Bay Lake. He set up what he called the Curtis Health

Alec driving the Model T, with boat behind and motor on the running board.

Center. Dr. Curtis came from Minneapolis for the summers and set up a Chiropractic Clinic in the building known as the "Annex," or the former Soule house.

Alec and his family also did all the office work necessary. They did their own advertising—mainly by word-of-mouth and wrote letters by hand. I remember sitting in the basement of our home in the winter and operating a robotyper machine. That machine ran on the same principle as a player piano, as it had a bellows.

In the winter, Alec became restless so he would get ideas of how to keep busy or make improvements. He got an idea of making signs lettered with clear-colored marbles in holes, backed by tin, that reflected headlights at night. That worked quite well, but had some drawbacks—some fell out of the holes. Scotchlite made the sign buttons obsolete. He also bought the formula for a septic tank cleaner, and the family spent the winter packaging the cleaner which Alec had advertised and took orders for. All resorters had septic tank problems, and this was their savior. It was soon discovered that yeast had the same result.

Alec was a very active person and made many advances and changes when he was the manager of Ruttger's Bay Lake Lodge. Jack returned from serving in the Army in 1955 and took over management of the property.

Lakeshore of Bay Lake Lodge on left.

Jack and Ann as Resort Operators

Jack, like his father before him, has been a very active manager. Many changes have occurred since he and Ann took over. The first summer that Jack was involved, there were new picture windows in the dining hall, the large lounge, and in all of the cottages replacing some of the shutters. All porches on cottages in shady areas were glassed in, and new thermostatic-controlled heaters were installed in all of the cottages. An activities director was hired to be in charge of tournaments and evening entertainment. By 1956, there were 36 cottages, and the dining room could accommodate 140 guests. In 1962, a new card room and a TV room had been built which doubled the size of the lobby. There were numerous

Ruttger Family: Front, L to R; Myrle, Mary, Ann; Back; Alec, Julia, Jack, and Chris.

changes and additions to cottages during the years. In 1967, a second tennis court was built, and both were resurfaced in green. New cottages were built replacing some that had been torn down or moved. In 1968, three new cottages were constructed, and the golf course was updated. In 1969, three more cottages were built after moving out three older ones, even with building costs up about 30 percent since 1967. In 1970, three new units were built to replace others that were moved out.

As you can see, there was a lot going on. In 1971, 109 acres of property were purchased to expand the golf course. That meant that all the land around Bass Lake and about 2,000 feet on Goose Lake were included. Plans were ready for the new nine-hole, 3,200 yard expansion. Late September in 1971, ground was broken for the new convention center/swimming pool complex. The complex opened on May 12, 1972, available to the public for a fee. The sports complex had an indoor pool, whirlpool in a tropical setting, sun lamps, lounges, exercise equipment, a pool table, Ping-Pong, and other games in a recreation room.

In the fall of 1973, Jack's family and Alec and Myrle stayed in Minnesota, a change from operating the motel in Florida. The resort was open for winter business beginning in the winters of 1972-1973 and 1973-1974. The 1974 energy crunch had more Minnesotans coming to Ruttger's. Two new tennis courts were completed in mid-August of 1974. In that same year, a four-unit complex was completed to replace two cottages that had burned down. By the spring of 1977, there was a complete irriga-

tion system for the entire golf course. The spring of 1978, there were two new tennis courts, making a total of six. The spring of 1980, four Sunset cottages were redone, and a new front desk was built. In 1981, there were 12 new lodge rooms for rent, a new kitchen, and a new dining room where the original kitchen had been—this dining room was called the Colonial Room. The convention complex and lodge buildings were connected, and a new front entrance was erected. Golf course condominiums were offered for sale in 1983. In 1986, the first nine holes of the new championship golf course were ready to play on. The annual fall Oktoberfest celebration was started in 1986. In 1987, there was a new dining room addition (the "New Log"), a new reception area, an entry area, and parking lot. Kids' Kamp was also new that year. The 16 villas were ready for occupancy the spring of 1990. This building was built where the original tennis courts had been just to the

west of the Alec Ruttger home place. By the spring of 1992, the new 18-hole championship golf course was completed. Jack's son, Christopher, officially took over the operation of Ruttger's Bay Lake Lodge on January 1, 1992. As you can see, Jack and Ann's term of operation covered many stages of development at the resort.

Many changes took place, including new cottages replacing older ones, cottages remodeled and enlarged. Picture windows were installed in place of shutters, additional and improved tennis courts, additional golf holes made available, a convention center and pool area, motel-type units, condominiums, additional dining space, a large registration area, and many more additions that could be recounted.

Now there are air conditioners and televisions in all units. The TVs are hooked up to cable which became available in the area in 1993. Improvements are ongoing. There is always something more to do.

Ruttger's wooden boats and white house, before 1934.

Chris as the Recently Appointed Resort Operator
—by Kay Bargen

Jack and Ann's son, Christopher, took over the operation of the resort on January 1, 1992. During the short period of time in which Chris has assumed leadership, he has implemented management principles appropriate to a growing organization. Chris has worked to bring the resort into

Chris Ruttger.

the '90s and beyond. Under his leadership, a complete computer system has been installed for use in all departments of the resort.

Of course, Chris had a lot of on-the-job training growing up on the resort and working in different areas of the operation. After a time of being independent of the resort following graduation from Cornell University, he returned to Ruttger's in 1988 in charge of dining, overseeing the menus, and seeing that the service was satisfactory.

Chris introduced the concept of team leadership. A management team has been formed and is working to achieve long-range goals. As the resort looks to its centennial year and the 21st century, it will work to be recognized around the world for its beautiful grounds, exceptional food, dedication to the environment, creative activities, and unequaled service with attention to detail.

The goal of the resort is to ensure every guest that their presence is appreciated and that their comfort is of primary concern. Chris and his staff will be carrying on the tradition, established by his great-grand parents, Joe and Josie, in 1898, of treating every guest like family. ℛ

Chapter Six

A Time Line of Bay Lake and Resort Developments

1736—The Ojibwe and Sioux started fighting over northern Minnesota lands.

1820—Fort Snelling was built.

1858—Minnesota became a state.

1860—Joseph was born in Germany and Josephine in Nauvoo, Illinois.

1862—The United States versus the Dakota Sioux conflict.

1865—The Civil War ended.

1870—Northern Pacific Railroad laid tracks as far as Deerwood, making travel easier to the Bay Lake area.

1871—A station stop established at Withington (later Deerwood).

1881—Joseph came to the United States.

1882—Cuyler Adams, David Archibald, and Robert Archibald cleared a path from Deerwood to Bay Lake—the first ever.

—The first permanent white settlers at Bay Lake—the very first was David Archibald.

—James D. Torrey and Asa Bennett set up sawmills on Bay Lake.

1883—S. H. Reif completed maps of Bay Lake.

—Henry Knieff and family moved to Bay Lake (wife Louisa, sister to Josephine).

1884—Iron ore was first mined in northeast Minnesota.

—The Bay Lake precinct was established, the Bay Lake School built, and a post office was established.

1886-1887—The Pioneer Co-op took over Bennett's sawmill, and workers began homesteading.

—Joseph Ruttger homesteaded the island on April 26, 1886.

1888—Edison invented the motion picture camera.

1889—Josephine Wasserzieher came to Bay Lake to stay with her sister, Louisa Knieff.

1890—Joseph and Josephine married on October 31st.

1892—Alexander John Ruttger was born on September 12th.

1894—Joseph and Josephine moved their family to the mainland, having bought property from J. S. Rankin.

—Maximillian (Max) Wilhelm Ruttger was born on September 15th.

1895—Josephine Ruttger was appointed postmistress of the Bay Lake post office.

—The first Fourth of July celebration took place at Bay Lake.

1896—Edward Adolph Ruttger was born on July 5th.

1898—The Spanish-American War began.

—The U.S. battleship Maine was attacked.

—The Bay Lake Summer Resort was established, with mostly fishermen as guests.

1899—William Joseph Ruttger was born on November 1st.

1900—A. F. Landstrom homesteaded what later became known as Church Island on Bay Lake.

1901—Myrle Fuller Ruttger was born on September 11th.

—Joe and Josie built their "Ruttger Cottage."

—Frank H. and Helen Bryant Below and three children came to Ruttger's starting family tourism.

1903—Orville and Wilbur Wright had their first successful flight.

1906—The Bay Lake Store was built by A.

N. Gray.

1908—Gus Klein from Duluth first came to Ruttger's with a fishing party (Dr. Harry Klein's father).

1909—The post office at Bay Lake closed due to the start of mail delivery.

1912—Alec graduated from high school in Duluth.

—Dr. Harry Klein of Duluth first came to Bay Lake with his parents. Daughter Gretchen is a close friend of the Ruttger family.

1914—Max Ruttger took over operation of the Bay Lake Store.

—Haas Ziegler first came to Bay Lake.

1917—The United States broke ties with Germany and declared war.

1918—Alec enlisted in the Army on February 2nd.

1919—A U. S. Navy seaplane made the first multi-stop transatlantic flight.

—Alec was out of the Army as of June 9th and went to Montana to homestead.

1920—Alec became operator of The Bay Lake Summer Resort.

—Alec married Minnie Marsh on May 23rd (Minnie died September 1923).

1921—The year of the building of Ruttger's private nine-hole golf course, built using a plan by H. H. Ziegler.

1922—The grand opening of Ruttger's log dining hall and lounge on June 22nd.

1924—Congressional action made all American Indians citizens.

—Alec married Myrle Margaret Fuller on September 14th.

1925—The Green Lantern night club and beach sports center was built.

1926—Mae Ruttger Heglund was born on September 14th.

1927—Charles Lindbergh flew nonstop to Paris—the first person to solo across the Atlantic Ocean.

1929—The stock market crashed and began America's worst depression.

—Alexander John (Jack) Ruttger Jr. was born on December 19th.

1930—Bill Ruttger took over operation of the Bay Lake Store.

—Max and Rosie built and started operating Ruttger's Pine Beach Lodge on Gull Lake.

1932—Bay Lake children were transported to Deerwood for schooling, ending the use of the Bay Lake schoolhouse for that purpose.

—Ann Hanlon Ruttger was born August 2nd.

1933—President Roosevelt ordered all banks closed.

1934—Jane Ruttger Bobich was born on August 29th.

—Bertha Pleidrup was hired as head cook of Ruttger's Bay Lake Lodge.

1935—The Social Security Act was passed by Congress.

—Ed and Eva Ruttger started operating Ruttger's Sherwood Forest Lodge near Gull and Margaret Lakes.

1936—Bill and Maudie built and started operating Ruttger's Shady Point Lodge on Whitefish Lake.

1937—Poland was invaded by Germany—U.S. declared neutrality.

—Don Ruttger, son of Max and Rosie, started operating Ruttger's Birchmont Lodge near Bemidji.

1939—The roadway that had run in front of Ruttger's property along the lake

was moved to the back of the property.

1941—Japan bombed Pearl Harbor, causing the U.S. to declare war.

—Ruby started working at Ruttger's Bay Lake Lodge.

1943—President Roosevelt approved the first payroll withholding tax.

—The Minnesota Resort Association was formed, with Alec the first president.

1945—Amy Pleidrup Downing was hired as baker.

1946—The U.N. General Assembly held its first session in London.

1947—Secretary of State Marshall proposed a plan for rebuilding Europe.

1948—Russia blockaded the Allies' sector of Berlin.

1951—Electric energy was produced from atomic power.

1953—Jack married Ann Hanlon on May 23rd.

1954—School segregation was ruled unconstitutional.

—Alexander John (Sandy) Ruttger III was born on November 2.

1955—Jack and Ann took over operation of Ruttger's Bay Lake Lodge.

—Lucia's first year as social hostess.

1956—The first transatlantic telephone call took place.

1957—The USSR launched Sputnik, the first earth satellite.

—Alec and Jack purchased the motel on Marathon Key in Florida in January.

—Julia Ann Ruttger was born on September 30.

1959—Castro became the Premier of Cuba.

1960—John Kennedy was elected President.

—Hurricane Donna hit Marathon Key on September 9th and did a lot of damage to the Ruttger Motel.

1962—Christopher Joseph Ruttger was born on January 28.

1963—John Kennedy was assassinated in Dallas.

1966—The government started Medicare for the elderly.

1967—It was Bertha's last year as cook at Ruttger's due to health problems.

—Mary Catherine Ruttger was born on November 27.

1968—Martin Luther King and Robert Kennedy were assassinated.

1969—Neil Armstrong was the first man on the moon.

—Sharon Simons became manager of the gift shops.

1970—It was Mary Heinrichs' first year as head cook.

1971—109 acres were purchased for golf course expansion.

—Late in September building started on the convention center complex.

1972—The multi-purpose complex opened on May 12th, including a convention center, swimming pool, recreation room, etc.

—Housing was readied for 50 persons for winter business.

1973—OPEC imposed a worldwide oil embargo.

—Alexander John III (Sandy) was killed in an accident in Miami, Florida.

1974—Nixon resigned as President of the U.S.

1976—The United States celebrated it's bicentennial year.

—The last year for Amy as baker.

1977—A complete irrigation system for the golf course was put in.
—Lynn Kehl was the new head cook as Mary Heinrichs retired.

1978—Myrle Ruttger died in February, and Alec died in May.

1979—Julie Ruttger married Perry Platisha on June 9.
—Al Cunningham was hired as grounds' supervisor.

1980—Sunset cottages were purchased and redone.
—Molly Ann Platisha was born.

1981—12 new lodge rooms, a new kitchen, and the Colonial Dining Room were constructed and ready for use.
—The convention complex and lodge buildings were connected, and there was a new front entrance.
—Blake Platisha was born.

1982—There was a deep recession both in the U.S. and abroad.

1983—The golf course condominiums were offered for sale.

1984—First year for Terry Dox as chef.
—Jordan Platisha was born.

1985—Expanded conference facilities to 10,000 square feet of meeting and banquet space.

1986—The space shuttle Challenger exploded killing all seven on board.
—Battle Point condominiums were purchased.
—The first annual Oktoberfest was celebrated.
—The first nine holes of the championship golf course were ready to play.

1987—The new log dining room was added, as well as a new reception area and parking lot.

—Barry Anderson became the general manager.
—Kids' Kamp was new, under direction of Edie Rue.

1988—Al Cunningham became the engineering and grounds manager.
—Greg Meyer began in the group sales department.
—Casey Platisha was born.

1990—Fred Bobich became the general manager.
—The villas were ready for occupation.

1992—Chris Ruttger became general manager of Ruttger's Bay Lake Lodge on January 1st.
—The new 18-hole championship golf course, The Lakes, was ready for use in the spring.
— A tree was dedicated to Ruby Treloar during Oktoberfest in honor of her 52 years of caring service.

1993—Fred Bobich became manager of Ruttger's Sugar Lake Lodge.
—Pat Kruper became the new golf course superintendent.
—A tree was planted in honor of Bertha and Amy at Oktoberfest.

1994—A new snack bar and grill was opened at the Pro Shop, overlooking Bass Lake and the 18th hole.
—Allison Mullen was hired as front office manager.
—Jack Ruttger received Outstanding Individual award from the Minnesota Office of Toursim.
—A tree was dedicated to Sally Ross, long-time housekeeper at Bay Lake and Florida Keys, at Oktoberfest.

1995—Mary Ruttger married Tom
   Witchger Jr. on April 29.
   —Ruby Treloar was named the 1995
   Outstanding Lodging Employee of
   the Year by the American Hotel &
   Motel Association.
1996—Perry Platisha left Ruttger's to form
   his own company -- Chad Gross
   was welcomed as the new
   controller.
   —Annette Kittock was hired to assist
   Chris in his many duties.
   —The tree at Oktoberfest was planted
   by Gretchen Klein in honor of all
   of our guests.
1997—The management team worked during the winter months to under-
   stand and articulate Ruttger's mission as it was established by Joseph
   and Josephine.
   —A new golf professional, Bill Laimer,
   and a resort services manager, Kelli
   Huxford, were hired.
   —A new computer system was
   installed.
   —The Sportswear Shop was converted
   to Auntie M's Kaffeehaus.
   —Bertha Pleidrup, our old-time cook
   and friend, died in March.
   —A tree was dedicated to A. J. (Sandy)
   Ruttger III during Oktoberfest.
1998—The new clubhouse, featuring Zig's
   Steakhouse and a new pro shop,
   opens in May.
   —The Lodge Nine is renamed Alec's
   Nine, in memory of Alec Ruttger's
   lifelong commitment to the game
   that began when he built the course
   in 1921.
   —The Centennial Celebration,
   Ruttger's Bay Lake Lodge celebrates
   its first 100 years. ℛ

Chapter Seven

The Resort's Development over Four Generations

Types of Units That Have Been Used for Housing Guests

According to writings that we have come across, the earliest housing for guests that came to stay at Ruttger's was in the barn haymow. Later they purchased tents. After they built their larger home, they housed people in rooms in that building as well as the "fishermen's house" constructed for that purpose. In addition, when Alec was manager, his family often stayed in tents in order to rent their space. I remember living in a room added on to our home, built just for summer living, so that summer guests could stay in our regular living quarters. The Joseph Ruttger home was built probably about 1901, as Uncle Bill said the last three boys were born in the tar-papered building that had been the Colony company store—apparently located just to the west of where Joe and Josie built their new house. I found an agreement between H. H. Ziegler and Joseph Ruttger dated July 27, 1914, leasing property for Zig to build a cabin, with the stipulation that after ten years the cabin would belong to Joseph Ruttger. This cabin is basically the same one as the present number 512, which of course has been totally remodeled. The "fishermen's house" was located just to the north of the Ruttger home. It had a social room with a fireplace on the main floor where people sat and told tall tales about their fishing

trips—and I am sure there were many as I have heard some. Besides, what else would there be to do with no television or movies to entertain them? I don't imagine there were many radios in those days. This building was later used for housing employees and given the name "the hen house." Then, when the convention center was built, the building was moved down the road to the Denny and Blanche Moore property and is now used as a horse barn.

When Alec took over management in 1920, he built 12 small cottages by the lake, and by 1956 there were 36 cottages that housed 140 guests. In 1981, the lodge rooms were built as part of the project when the new kitchen and Colonial Dining Room were built. At that time the convention complex and main-lodge buildings were connected. The resort bought the Sunset property in 1980, which included some cabins, and is located just to the east

H. H. Ziegler's Cottage, currently number 512.

Ed, Max, Alec, and Bill (in front) Ruttger. 1901, the constuction of the Ruttger house was in progress. It turned out to be the cornerstone of the lodge.

of the original property. Golf course condominiums were offered for sale through Ruttger and Ruttger Realty in 1983 to be rented by the resort. The Battle Point condominiums were purchased in 1986 and are located on Bay Lake about one-and-a-half miles east of the main resort property. The total possible capacity today is about 350 guests.

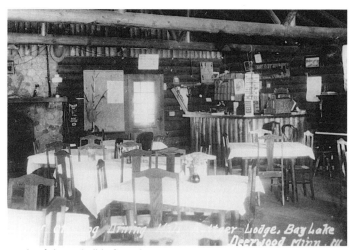

Inside of dining hall before electricity.

History of the Old Log Dining Room

When Alec returned from France following the First World War and after his try at ranching in Montana, he took over operation of the resort at his parents' request. In 1922, he decided there was need for a larger dining room. At that time there was only a small dining space, a part of the main house and porches. They set about building the present original section of the log dining hall. In the planning, this construction was to be 40 feet by 50 feet in size. Peter Brand, a local log carpenter, was engaged to be in charge of construction. Pete insisted they build using poplar logs for the walls, guaranteeing that if they gave the roof a projection of four feet the poplar logs would last indefinitely, but if the projection were small, the logs would rot in a short time. Those logs did last a very long time, as there was no need for repairs until 1985. Many of the 54-foot poplar logs were cut and skidded from steep hills and hollows three miles north of the resort in the Placid Lake area known as the Devil's Washboard by early natives. The steep hollows made the trees grow straight and tall reaching for sunlight.

Peter Brand.

To build with logs it was necessary to have eight corner men—two men for each corner. A log would be placed directly over the bottom log, then scribed with a compass, whereupon the bottom of the top log would be cut in a "V" fashion to conform to the irregularities of the top of the bottom log, in order to make an almost perfect fit to keep out the wind and weather. All of this was done by hand and winch (not with chainsaws or tractors with front loaders). The corners did require expert log men to execute a close fit. We received information

Inside of dining hall after electricity.

The fireplace lobby back then. Fremont Ditty and Alec Ruttger behind desk and Joseph Ruttger sitting, looking at you. Note the dog on the table at bottom right.

about Peter Brand from his son, Carl. He said his father must have been about 62 years of age at the time he built the dining hall. He also said his father had built the Green Lantern, the first cabins, and possibly other buildings on the Ruttger property.

View of the outside of the log dining hall, from the north.

The steamboat ferry was used to transport people across the lake, as roads were not very good in those days. Edward Wasserzieher was the pilot. L-R: Edward, Otto (father), Adele (mother), the other person is unidentified.

History of Sunset Cabins and Steamboat

Edward Wasserzieher, nephew of Josephine Ruttger, bought property just to the east of the Ruttger establishment, which became known as Sunset. He had his home on Echo Lake which is now called Tame Fish Lake. He bought the property in order to operate and beach a screw-drive steamboat on Bay Lake, used to ferry people across the lake. He had built a drawbridge over the creek between Bay Lake and Echo Lake so he could get back home. Uncle Bill said Edward had a pulley and had horses do the pulling in order to lift the bridge. In those days the water was considerably higher than it is now, making for passage down the creek. That creek was known as Mud River and later named Ripple River. The steamboat was probably the first of that type on Bay Lake. It is possible that A. A. Miller used that type of boat for moving his log booms, but most certainly the Wasserzieher steamboat was the first screw-driven boat on Bay Lake. The Bay Lake property used for the steamboat landing was later used as the home of Edward and his family where they also started a housekeeping cottage resort. In 1980, Jack purchased the property and cottages, and they are now included as part of Ruttger's Bay Lake Lodge and still known in the area as Sunset.

The Ice House

—by Jack Ruttger

From the turn of the century until about 1950, if you wanted ice for your water or to keep your "ice box" cool, you needed Bay Lake ice. In the winter, a crew of Bay Lakers made their living by cutting ice for inhabitants around the lake. It was a cold, very heavy job that those men performed, and if they ever misstepped when pulling a "cake" of ice from the water, they would not last. Before the gasoline engine came onto the scene at Bay Lake in the early 30s, they cut the 24 inch to 30 inch thick ice by hand. As a child, I recall watching them cut the ice into cakes about two feet by three feet and worrying that they would be standing on one when cutting and go into the water. It certainly wouldn't be like a dip in Bay Lake in July! Later in the 1930s, these men rigged up a gas-powered saw rig, similar to those used to cut wood. The 100-pound blocks of ice were floated in the open water and men with long-handled ice tongs would then pull them out. They wore cleats, and with a chisel they notched the ice by the open water so they could get a good footing. Sixty years later I still shudder when I think of what would have happened if one of them had

Loading ice cakes into the ice house.

Taking the ice cakes out of the lake.

slipped and gone into the freezing water.

Since nobody had a tractor or a truck in the early days, it was by horse-drawn sleigh that ice was taken to the "ice house." At Ruttger's they would stack the ice in 12-15 layers—enough to last for a year. The bottom layer was relatively easy to load, and from there on it got harder and harder. The picture on page 85 shows the men sliding a cake of ice up the steel runners.

How could you keep ice through those hot July days? Sawdust from a local mill was packed a foot high over the top and around the sides. By Labor Day we were down to the last tier, and the ice cakes had shrunk very little.

The ice was used for the kitchen "ice boxes" and for the drinking water in the dining room. Yes, clean, drinkable Bay Lake water was served as crushed ice to the paying guests. An attempt was made to wash the ice thoroughly, but often people in the dining room would pick a piece of sawdust from their water or iced tea—never a complaint.

Here is an interesting point to think about: when people caught fish, they were stored on that same ice in the ice house until being cleaned, or some had them "gilled and gutted," then stored in preparation for taking them home.

The cakes of ice were chiseled into three parts. The grinder took a while to get rotating, but once it did it chewed up the chunks easily. Old-timers still remember the early-morning sound of crushing ice.

Electrical refrigeration and ice cubers were yet to come in those days. You wouldn't drink the water from Bay Lake or any lake today. There was never a thought about it then, and I never knew of anyone getting sick from the lake water. I recall when we were kids, we would skate before the snows came and the ice was but three to four inches thick. We would get thirsty, and with the heel of our skates we would chop a hole in the ice and drink good old Bay Lake water.

The old ice grinder presently sits by the Country Store. ℛ

Chapter Eight

Recreational Attractions at Ruttger's Bay Lake Lodge

Fishing, the First Recreation

—by Jack Ruttger

From our beginning, fishing has been an important part of our business. The huge string of fish shown in this picture is no longer possible, here nor most likely any place else in the world. We have often wondered what was done with that large number of fish considering the lack of electrical refrigeration in those days. Our thinking is that those not eaten right away were kept on ice or smoked. (See the story on the ice house.)

Today, Bay Lake is most noted for its bass fishing, although northern pike and panfish are also plentiful. The fish in the picture shown are almost all walleyes. They are not as plentiful now as the sporty bass. There have been fishing guides working out of Ruttger's Lodge since the late 20s or early 30s. During the 1940s, there were as many as seven guides at one time working to show Ruttger guests where the lunker bass were. We advertised that we fished 100 lakes within a ten-mile radius of the lodge in the 40s and 50s.

Grandmother Josie used her special batter when cooking those fresh fish back at the turn of the century. She was noted for her fine meals and especially her German dishes. To this day, fish is a very popular item on the menu, and we do prepare fresh-caught fish for people when we are asked. The batter has changed a little, some say for the better. I doubt that we could ever better the

H.H. Ziegler with his catch of walleyes from Bay Lake in the 1920s.

1945, Ted Bateman, guide, second from left with his fishing party, Mr. and Mrs. Dyer and Larry Wolfe.

Bill Cole, guide in the 60s and 70s.

taste of Grandmother Josie's fresh-fried fish to those who ate them back at the turn of the century.

The most noted guides were Gil Lyman in the 1930s and the Batemans from the late 30s up until the early 50s. The Batemans were brothers, Frank and Bob (Pops), and also Pops' son, Ted. Ted

Ruttger guests displaying their catch in the late 30s or early 40s.

was by far the favorite guide of all we had! At 4:00 a.m., Ted would arrive at the back door of the lodge kitchen, gain entry, then prepare breakfast for his "party" for that morning. By sunrise, they were on one of Ted's secret little lakes close by. By 11:00 a.m., they were back displaying a rack full of beautiful large-mouth bass. Nobody

Dan Johnson, Salina, Kansas, in the 60s. Nice string of fish!

Darrell Hollister, Chicago, with a six-pound bass. 1967.

could catch fish or lead their party to the fishing holes better than Ted.

As fishing was so important to the resort's business, Alec Ruttger became very involved in the propagation of fish in all of our lakes. He worked closely with Dr. Samuel Eddy, a professor from the University of Minnesota Forestry School, on bettering the fishing in our lakes.

Fishing is not the attraction today that it was back in the early days, but it is still popular. Several guides from the area work out of the resort. It seems

Gil Lyman, guide in the 30s and 40s.

that most people ask where the good spots are, and they take a son, daughter, or grandchild with them and go out to commune with nature. Fishing today is as good as it was back in the 40s and 50s, because of better conservation practices. Today, the prize is often weighed, pictured, and returned to reproduce. Just enough are taken for the table. The thrill is the tug on the line, the solitude of being on a lake with a wooded shoreline, and the absence of worries altogether. They disappear the moment you set your foot into a boat. The stringer full of fish is no longer the sign of a good fishing experience. There is much more to enjoy on that trip, and those memories are lasting. Picture a five-pound bass striking your lure, cast toward a tree-lined shore. Out of the water it comes, not once, but

L to R: Frank, Ted, and Pops Bateman.

three or four times, trying to shake the hook. Finally, the fish is in the boat and the fun is over. Back into the water it goes to make more enjoyable experiences for future generations. Fishing isn't just taking fish—it's a total memorable experience!!

Pops Bateman, Art Dewing, gardener, and Frank Bateman, 1946.

Alec Ruttger - obviously, no limit. A mixture of bass and walleyes from Bay Lake.

Golf and Its Development

—by Jack Ruttger

It is fair to say that not many northern Minnesota resorts had golf as an amenity in 1921. Ruttger's at Bay Lake did. Alec Ruttger was just back from a homesteading stint in Montana deciding that Bay Lake was really where he wanted to be. The resort business was more to his liking than ranching, and so with his journey in the Army overseas in World War I complete, he set about developing the resort.

Number 1 Tee. The tee shot was across the county road. Note the dress of the gentlemen and ladies.

With fishing so fabulous in those days and so few people playing golf, why would he agree to such a project? Well, there was a guest who spent his summers at Ruttger's by the name of Haas Ziegler, "Zig" for short. Zig vacationed in California during the winter of 1920, where he was introduced to golf. Zig convinced Alec that the cow pasture should be a

Note the sand greens. This shot was taken looking to the northeast. Today the practice green on the Lodge Nine would be in the foreground.

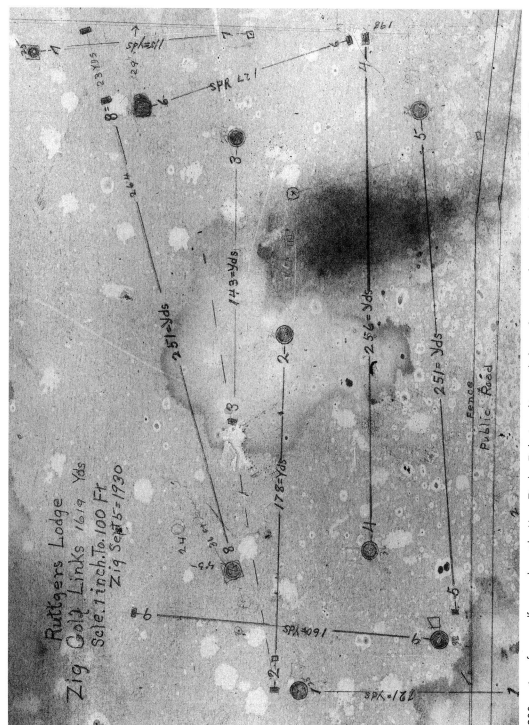

1930 routing of new golf course layout by Haas Ziegler. Today's architectural plans take reams of paper and thousands of dollars. This routing was done on cardboard tacked to a piece of wood.

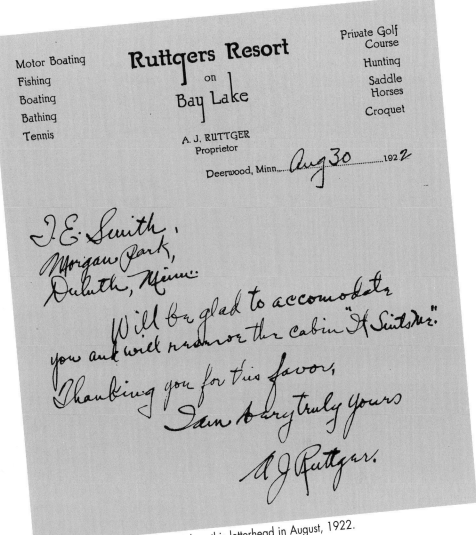

Motor Boating
Fishing
Boating
Bathing
Tennis

Ruttgers Resort
on
Bay Lake

Private Golf
Course
Hunting
Saddle
Horses
Croquet

A. J. RUTTGER
Proprietor

Deerwood, Minn., Aug 30 1922

J. E. Smith,
Morgan Park,
Duluth, Minn:

Will be glad to accomodate you and will reserve the cabin "It Suits Her".

Thanking you for this favor,

I am very truly yours

A J Ruttger.

"Private Golf Course" is advertised on this letterhead in August, 1922.

Alec Ruttger on the left, 1930.

golf course. Four sand greens and nine tees were made during that summer. One green would service several tees, and some fairways crossed one another, with the first tee-off crossing the highway. Ponies and cows "mowed" the grass. Crank-case oil from a filling station was used to make the sand greens firm. Thus golf was part of the vacation package in 1921, and it has been ever since.

Jim Halls of Edina, Minnesota, has had three holes in one at Ruttger's.

In 1930, Zig became a golf course architect of sorts and did the routing for a course expansion (see page 93). The ponies and cows also enjoyed the links, but were not allowed on the greens—they were fenced. That was the start of our nine-hole golf course, a course that is still popular today after many revampings. The greens now are bent grass, some are where Zig laid them out, and other parts of the original course can be seen, like the knoll in the middle of number two fairway.

When the new 18-hole championship course was built ten years ago, there were reams of paper that the architects and engineers needed. Zig used a piece of cardboard, a straight edge, and a pencil. The cost to build that course was probably under $5,000, counting the 1930 "expansion" to nine greens. Our new 18-hole course was in excess of a million dollars. Are 18 holes of championship golf and the nine-hole course enough golf? Probably not. A parcel of land was just purchased in anticipation that more golf will be needed soon.

How times have changed! We have gone from sand greens and tees to bent grass greens and blue grass tees, from wood shafted clubs to graphite, from real wood drivers to metal "woods," and, of course, from walking the course for exercise to fancy golf carts with sun tops to protect you from the weather. In the early days, people would try golf when the day's fishing was over—now, people try fishing when the day's golf is over.

Starting a golf course at a northern Minnesota resort in 1921, when fishing was unbelievable, was something that nobody else had done in Minnesota. Those of us who grew up with Alec Ruttger know he was always on the leading edge in developing Ruttger's Bay Lake Lodge during his era.

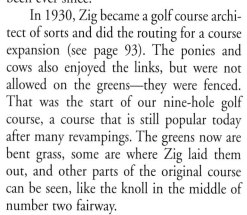

Footnote:
Zig made a hole-in-one one day. He told Joe about it and Joe didn't seem to be impressed, saying it was "damned fool luck." Joe and Zig got into an argument and didn't talk to each other for the rest of that summer.

Horseback Riding

—by Mae

I can remember horses that were owned by the resort and used for guests to ride. As I recall, there were just a few, and those did pretty much as they chose—there were numerous instances where the horse would decide it had enough and would run back to the barn. We kids (Jack, Jane, and I) were very involved at the stable when Cowboy Bill Sanderson brought his horses to rent out from the resort. Cowboy Bill lived in Hibbing and brought the horses by truck in the spring. He must have rented horses at the resort for two or three years, probably about 1935 through 1937. We thought he was the greatest, and he gave each of us a pair of cowboy chaps as a gift. We sure did strut when we wore those chaps.

When Cowboy Bill came to the resort, there was a large farm barn that he used to store his riding equipment and house his horses. One night someone apparently had too much to drink at the Green Lantern and went into the haymow to sleep. It was decided he had been smoking, the hay caught on fire, and the barn burned. Fortunately no person or horse was lost in the fire.

The next person to bring riding horses to the resort for the summer was Howard Curtis. He had horses at Carlton College in the winter and had students ride them from Northfield, Minnesota, to Bay Lake in the spring. Howard used English saddles, and that is what I learned on. At times, business would be rather slow so Howard and some of the college girls that worked with him would practice jumping.

Mae, Jack, Jane, and Cowboy Bill.

Denny and Blanche Moore.

Cowboy Bill, horses and friends. Joe Ruttger, second from left; Jack Ruttger, next to him; and Cowboy Bill to his left.

I rode enough, so became one of the "guides" that went with guests. We used to ride on some of the roads in the area, such as the road to Placid and Peterson Lakes. Sometimes we went to Battle Point. There was very little traffic in those days so there was no danger from being on the highways.

Howard probably had about a dozen horses that he rented out, and I would guess that he was here the years of 1938 to 1942. Blanche and Denny Moore knew Howard, and when he stopped coming to the resort they started bringing their horses by truck each spring for a number of years. They eventually moved to the "rock house" just to the north of the golf course entrance. Their horses were rented out of the stable at the resort from about 1943 until 1986, when insurance companies decided the risk was too high. Blanche's horses were ridden on trails behind the golf course, and the paths went deeper and deeper into the soil over those many years. It was sad to see an era pass.

The kiddies all ride at Ruttger's Bay Lake Lodge.

Watersports and Equipment
—by Mae

There has always been great concern about making the lakefront appealing to people coming to the resort. In a letter written by Alec the spring of 1933, he said they had improved the bathing beach.

Watersports and activities have been a part of Ruttger's for many years, starting with the swimming and fishing done by the early visitors. Then in the 1920s, there was the use of motors on boats, some for fishing and a larger one for pleasure. During the 1940s, the sport of water-skiing began and by the mid-1950s was very popular at

Ruttger's. Jack Ruttger was very good at doing tricks on water skis, including bare-foot skiing and going over jumps. Joe Simons, a part of Ruttger's since 1955, remembers the fun he and John Chenoweth, guest, had skiing every day, except when it was storming.

There were a number of years when Ruttger's put on a water show every Saturday afternoon during the summer months. Guests that were qualified, employees, and family members were included in the show. People from around the area used to come to

Jack Ruttger.

Fred Bobich and Sandy Ruttger, cousins, 1965.

Daredevil stunts were always a part of Ruttger's water shows on Saturdays.

Clowns, Jack Ruttger and Joe Simons, always made the audience laugh.

see the shows. There was a pyramid of skiers, with some riding shoulders, a jump set up for exhibition jumps, as well as a clown act, and then also a routine put on in the outdoor pool. Joe Simons, long-time employee and friend, says he remembers being in the pyramids. One year they tried the seven-man pyramid and just about killed themselves on that one. Joe's mother, Lucia, did the announcing and made the show interesting. Joe remembers the clown acts they did. He also remembered Jack's son, Sandy, and nephew, Fred, taking off from the beach on little shoe skis and then barefoot. ℛ

A sample of a Saturday afternoon water show – the Flag Act. Employees were taught to ski in the show.

Chapter Nine
An Account of the Bay Lake Store and Shops

The first store on property was The Bay Lake Store which is now Ruttger's Country Store. It was built and operated as a grocery and feed store for the neighborhood to buy their supplies. Mr. A. N. Gray built the original store in 1906. He operated it until Max Ruttger bought it, and he was proprietor from 1914 to 1930 at which time his brother, Bill, took over. Bill ran the store from 1930 until 1936. From 1936 until 1939 the store was managed by Drexel Geist, from 1939 to 1946 it was managed by John Andolshek, and from 1946 to 1951 "Loki" Lundgren and his family were in charge. After that time, the store was owned by Ruttger's and sometimes leased by others until 1971. That year it was stated in the Ruttger Reporter that the store was to be used for early and late conventions and movies, as well as other activities for summer guests. This plan was put in place until

Max Ruttger, store proprietor.

The Bay Lake Store, 1906. Currently Ruttger's Country Store.

The Bay Lake store and garage.

The first Paul Bunyan Trading Post.

a convention hall was built in 1972. The store had most recently been used as a tavern before being returned to Ruttger management.

A gift-bait shop was built just across from the former Alec Ruttger home in about 1950. It was known as The Paul Bunyan Trading Post. The front half of the store was used for gifts, jewelry, and fishing tackle and baits. The back half of the store was used for

Paul Bunyan activity room, our first meeting room.

an activities room, with a Ping Pong table, a table bowling alley, and benches set up for movies and talent shows. This would probably accommodate about 75 people at most. It was also the first attempt at having a place for group meetings—not very comfortable or spacious.

In about 1954, a new Paul Bunyan Trading Post was built across from the Miller garage. It later became Corner Sportswear and then Auntie M's Kaffeehaus. The original Paul Bunyan Trading Post was then used as a dormitory to house young women working at the lodge. When the convention center was built, the original Paul Bunyan Trading Post was torn down to make way for the new construction.

The Bay Lake Country Store was restored in 1988 with the tin ceiling and maple flooring uncovered and refreshed. ◆

The new Paul Bunyan Trading Post and Pro Shop, 1954.

Chapter Ten
The Green Lantern Chronicle

The front of the Green Lantern and the toboggan slide, located at the west side of the resort property. The pilings still stand.

Uncle Bill Ruttger said that as close as he could remember the Green Lantern was built in the year 1925. The dance club and soda fountain was built very close to Bay Lake, and part of it even extended over the water. The July 1929 issue of the <u>American Resort</u> magazine stated that there were dances every Tuesday, Thursday, and Saturday put on by an excellent orchestra. The same orchestra played every weekday evening and on Sunday noon for dinners in the log dining hall at Ruttger's. The University of Minnesota orchestra also played there.

The Green Lantern was well-known in the Bay Lake area, as well as surrounding towns. The Crosby-Ironton High School had many senior class picnics at that location with the lake to swim and boat on. I have heard of romances that began as a result of meeting at dances there. My mother's sister, Edith, said she and her husband of 60 years, Fritz Tully, met at a dance at the Green Lantern. Fritz said he was playing the violin with the Merry Makers when Edith came to dance. He played with the group for two or three years; he remembers that Charlie

The east side of the Green Lantern and toboggan slide.

The dance floor of the Green Lantern. The famous Carroll Carpenter band.

Osterheim, Harold Hamilton, and Adolph Prushek were in the same band with Adolph playing the drums. In the 20s and 30s, the Green Lantern was very popular and featured name bands including Carroll Carpenter and Norbie Mulligan. Even at this time people ask at Ruttger's about the Green Lantern. Carpenter and Mulligan's names are still heard each summer.

The resort finally decided to stop having dances following the season of 1941. It was announced in the Lodge spring letter dated May 8, 1942, that the Green Lantern would no longer have dances due to the noise that occurred. Cottages had been built quite close to the Lantern, and there was a lot of noise following dances on through the night. Sometimes people went swimming or just stayed around the area for a noisy time. Today the pilings for the Green Lantern may be seen on the west shore of the property. ℛ

Tennis court in the foreground with the Green Lantern in the background. Note the well-dressed tennis players.

Chapter Eleven

Ruttger's German Heritage and the Beginning of Oktoberfest

German Heritage

Jack and Ann Ruttger visited the Rüttger winery in Neuleiningen, Germany. Jack has related the story of the location and our importing of wines. "Deep in the Rhine River wine country atop a knoll sits a little picturesque town named Neuleiningen, home of the Rüttger family and the winery they established in 1643. We have mastered the hurdles of importing the wine from the family. We are the only source of Rüttger wine in America from the Rudi Rüttger Weinkellerei, now operated by his son, Heinrich, and family. Rudi Rüttger was the cousin of Alec Ruttger. Alec and Rudi's fathers were cousins in the Neuleiningen family located 20 miles west of Mannheim, Germany. Rudi's family remained in Europe while grandfather Joseph Ruttger emigrated to the U.S. in 1881 and eventually settled the Bay Lake Lodge site."

During the 1940s, the families corresponded frequently, and care packages were sent abroad to help ease the war's effects. It was not until 1982, however, that Jack first ventured overseas to the home place to meet relatives and see the winery firsthand. Jack was interested in the possibility of importing some of the over 50 varieties; myriad

The front cover of Rüttger's wine list.

In the Rüttger Vineyards in Neuleiningen, Germany. October 4, 1997. Heinrich and Jack Ruttger.

channels were explored. The eventual arrival of the five selected wines in the first shipment came after involvement by the German Consul, a Chicago importer, and a St. Paul connection. The reaction to these wines by guests and visitors has been outstanding.

Development of Oktoberfest

The first annual Oktoberfest celebration was held at Ruttger's on a weekend in October in 1986. This has been a very popular event and has been well-attended each year since. One of the big attractions, in addition to just being there for the weekend, is the quality craft fair with over 100 artists and crafters. German entertainers play in bands, dance, and sing for the guests. Jugglers, clowns, and magicians stroll the grounds to add to the festivities. German food is available in the dining

L. to R.: Ann Ruttger, Heinrich and Theresa Rüttger, Emma (Mrs. Rudi) Rüttger, and Katherina Rüttger taken October 2, 1997, at the Rüttger winery.

room on Friday and Saturday evenings, as well as booths that furnish food and beverage on Saturday afternoon. Ruttger employees appear in German dress to make the occasion more festive. ℛ

Alphorns.

Jack Ruttger and Jim Roehl.

Bavarian Club Enzian dancers.

Saturday night dance.

Concord Singers from New Ulm, Minnesota.

Chapter Twelve

Many Present and Past Employees Enhance the Resort

Advertising, Office, and Reservations.

Alec was always a great believer in advertising and made many efforts to promote Ruttger's. He attended tourism shows in cities, passing out literature to advertise Ruttger's Bay Lake Lodge, as well as to advertise for his own certain locality—Bay Lake, Cuyuna Range, Brainerd Lakes, Arrowhead, or Minnesota if out-of-state. Of course, ads were put in newspapers in Oklahoma, Kansas, Missouri, Chicago, and Minneapolis, St. Paul, and Duluth.

An article written in the <u>Brainerd Dispatch</u> on November 27, 1933, stated that Alec Ruttger had visited Florida to investigate a new means to publicize the area. Alec was quoted as saying he "anticipated there would be increased business due to the improvement of state trunk highway number 18."

Early employees, Sally and Tollef (better known as Birke) Birkeland, worked for many years in the late 30s and early 40s in the offices and reservation correspondence areas. They worked during their summer break from teaching school in Waconia. Eventually they moved to Bay Lake and started their own resort, Birkeland's Bay Lake Lodge. They were good personal friends of Alec and Myrle.

Housekeeping and Maintenance

At first the Ruttger family must have done the cleaning where

Tollef and Sally Birkeland.

their guests were housed and fed. Then as time went on and the need arose, local girls were hired to help out.

One of our most beloved friends was Sally Ross who ran our housekeeping for 25 years. Sally finished at Bay Lake in October, took a month off, then was off to Florida to handle our housekeeping there. She had blazing red hair and a smile from ear-to-ear. Employees and guests loved Sally, as did all of the Ruttger family. Sally passed away in 1978 while working at our resort in Florida. We planted a tree in her memory at the Oktoberfest in 1994.

Today our housekeeping is overseen by Al Cunningham who has been an employee since 1979. Al

Sally Ross

Al Cunningham working in the Ruttger gardens.

his day he would hum religious songs. On Sunday he would rest by going to three or four church services. He was truly a man to remember forever at Ruttger's. "Oh! that so?" was his stock reply to any statement made to him.

Footnote:
Alec Ruttger is remembered for his handful of sticks and papers that he had picked up, "my business is picking up," he would say.

also manages maintenance, grounds, and landscaping. The grounds are immaculate, the maintenance of the property is near perfect, and rooms are always tip-top. He carries on our mission of cleanliness.

Art of All Trades

Art Dewing, employment from 1941-1960, was a faithful employee until the end of his life. What a good-hearted character! He did everything there was to do outside, and he did it alone. Gardening, lawn mowing, garbage hauling, painting, fish cleaning, and boat rentals were among his duties. Today there are 20 people doing these jobs that he once did alone. Art started his day at 5:00 a.m. and finished at sundown. He loved to do his gardening early. Six days a week for 20 years he made the place look great, and all during

Art Dewing, faithful employee of Ruttger's.

Cooks and Recipes through the Years

There have been many recipes used in preparing food for the palates of guests through the years.

Josephine's—Unfortunately, we do not have many of Josie's as we have not come across a cookbook that was hers—if indeed there was one. Some of her recipes were handed down to her family, and we have three that we will list here. I would guess that many foods cooked were prepared from experience, with the use of a pinch of this and a handful of that.

BLUEBERRY BUCKLE

Mix together thoroughly:
>¾ cup sugar
>¼ cup soft shortening
>1 egg

Stir in:
>½ cup milk

Sift together and stir in:
>2 cups sifted flour
>2 tsp. baking powder
>½ tsp. salt

Carefully blend in before putting into pan:
>1 cup blueberries

Spread batter in a greased and floured 9" square pan and sprinkle with the following topping (crumb mixture):

Mix together:
>½ cup sugar
>⅓ cup sifted flour
>½ tsp. cinnamon
>¼ cup soft butter

Bake 45 to 50 minutes in 375 degree oven. Serve warm and fresh from the oven.

PENNY MUFFINS

>2 large cups of water
>1 yeast cake
>½ cup sugar
>2 Tbsp. lard
>2 eggs
>Salt to taste

Mix flour in to form a soft dough at noon. Poke down at supper time and put in a greased pan and cover at bedtime. Bake for breakfast. Put the dough that is left in a cool place until wanted.

Sisters, Bertha and Amy, preparing a meal for Ruttger guests. From the Pleidrup family in Verndale, Minnesota.

DOUGHNUTS

½ cup thick sour cream
1 large cup buttermilk
2 eggs
1 cup sugar
1 level tsp. soda
1 tsp. baking powder
1 tsp. nutmeg
Add flour to make a soft dough.

Bertha and Amy's Recipes—

Bertha and Amy were sisters who worked at Ruttger's Lodge for many years—Bertha as the head cook for 34 years and Amy as the baker for 31. They were well-known for their cooking and baking, as well as their personal characteristics. Bertha was a very hard-working person, who had been raised on a farm and learned her trade from cooking at home. She worked at a sorority at the University of Minnesota during winters. She was always searching for new recipes and had a variety to work from. She was a determined person. Former workers still remember her giving orders for them to quiet down. Amy, the baker, always had someone in her little corner. She enjoyed talking to people and always had her egg-coffee ready. Jack's children all remember that when they were small Amy used to have them sit on a stool near her while she would feed them cookies, brownies, or some other goodies. She always said they were good for them as they had eggs and milk in them. Bertha retired in 1967 and Amy in 1976, and we give them credit for setting the goals for our food service that we will never waver from. They demanded quality with no waste. Discipline in the kitchen and dining room was a must. That is still our mission and will be forever.

BERTHA'S ALBONDIGO SOUP

1 Tbsp. bacon fat
½ cup chopped onion
1 can hominy, drained
2 cups tomatoes
3 cups chicken or beef stock
½ lb. ground beef
½ cup minced onion
¼ cup cornmeal
½ clove garlic, minced
½ tsp. salt
1 egg, beaten
Freshly ground black pepper

In heavy soup kettle, brown the onion and hominy in the bacon fat. Add tomatoes and stock to this and bring to a boil. If you do not have stock, you may use canned bouillon. Mix together the ground beef, cornmeal, minced garlic, onion, salt, pepper, and beaten egg. Form into tiny balls and drop in the boiling soup. Lower heat and simmer for 1 hour.

BERTHA'S BOILED SALAD DRESSING

½ cup sugar
2 tsp. flour
1 tsp. dry mustard
1 tsp. salt
½ cup vinegar
½ cup cold water
2 whole eggs or 5 egg yolks

Mix sugar, flour, and salt. Add vinegar and water and beat. When hot, pour over beaten eggs and cook until thick in top of double-boiler. When ready to use, thin with sweet, sour, or whipped cream. This will keep a long time.

Amy's Brownies

½ cup margarine
1 cup sugar
2 eggs, beaten slightly
1 tsp. vanilla
⅔ cup sifted flour
2 squares bitter chocolate, melted
½ cup chopped nut meats

Mix all ingredients, adding chocolate and nut meats last. Use 8-inch pan, lined with wax paper. Bake at 325 degrees 25 minutes. Do not over bake. To have "under baked" is part of the secret. Grease the pan, line with wax paper, grease it, and dust with flour and shake off the excess. Wait about 5 minutes after taking out of oven, then tip out of pan. Frost with powdered sugar icing, either white or chocolate.

Killarney Cookies

2 squares chocolate
1 can Borden's sweetened milk
1 cup crushed dry cake crumbs
½ cup nut meats
Pinch of salt
1 tsp. vanilla

Melt chocolate with milk in top of double-boiler until thick. Add crumbs, nut meats, and vanilla. Blend well. Drop on greased cookie sheet. Bake in 350 degree oven for 10 minutes.

Amy's Rolls

This may be used for plain dinner rolls, wiener buns, hamburger buns, or CARAMEL ROLLS.

2 cups potato water
2 cups warm milk
1 cup lard
5 eggs
¾ cup white sugar
4 cups or more flour

1 tsp. salt
1 Tbsp. brown sugar
¼ cup warm water
2 packages yeast

Cream lard, add sugar, eggs, and salt; add liquid. Add 4 cups white flour, then the yeast liquid. Continue to add flour until the dough is soft and easy to handle. Work in pan or on floured board. Grease bowl with oil and put dough into it until it rises to double, in a warm place, free from draft. Put on floured board and shape into desired shapes. CARAMEL ROLLS: With shortening spread on pan until white, put brown sugar on this and shake well, but do not leave more on than sticks. Shape as desired. Amy cut hers into strips, rolled in cinnamon-sugar mixture and shaped round, like a pinwheel. Let rise. Bake 18-19 minutes in a 380 to 400 degree oven.

French Donuts

1 cup water
1 cup flour
1 Tbsp. lard
1 tsp. salt
1 cup eggs

Bring water to a boil, add the lard, salt, and stir in the flour until all the lumps are stirred out. Put in mixer at high speed. Add one egg at a time. Cut brown paper (or locker paper) to fit fryer. Grease well. Put donut dough in pastry bag and shape. Heat oil to 370 degrees. Turn donuts into this and turn as soon as they start to split. Then turn and they will split again; then turn again. Drain on a wire rack. Let cool and frost with powdered sugar icing.

Sisky Donuts

1 yeast cake
½ cup lukewarm cream

1 cup sugar
4 eggs, beaten
¾ cup butter
2 Tbsp. sugar
1 cup cream, heated
½ tsp. salt
2 tsp. rum
4-5 cups flour

Dissolve yeast in lukewarm cream and the 2 Tbsp. sugar. Combine sugar, butter, heated cream, salt, and rum. Add 2 cups of flour and then the yeast mixture and beat. Stir in the eggs and beat. Add flour to make a soft dough and mix until smooth. Let rise until double. Put on floured board, cut ½-inch thick. Let rise about 10 minutes. Deep fry in oil at 350 degrees. This dough may be refrigerated overnight.

Chef Terry Dox.

Chef Terry Dox—Our qualified head chef is Terry Dox, who started cooking at Ruttger's in 1984. Terry carries on the Ruttger tradition of putting food-quality first. That's where our emphasis has always been, and with his talent, energy, and leadership we are rising to new levels. The numbers are vastly different today. In the 40s and 50s we served 130 people at a meal. In the 60s and 70s, 140 to 150. Now we serve 300 to sometimes 800 in high season. Our kitchen equipment is modern and our food service is very efficient. Terry keeps current on all food-service matters by attending seminars in the winter. In the winter of 1996-97, he learned sauce and herb cooking techniques at the Culinary Institute of America in the Napa Valley of California. Terry is quite a person to watch, as every move counts—and he never shows stress when there is a change in plans or numbers. The resort put out a cookbook in 1990 with many of Terry's recipes included.

WILD RICE SOUP

4 stalks celery, chopped fine
2 onions, chopped fine
8 oz. fresh mushrooms, chopped fine
1 whole chicken, cooked and chopped
2 pints cream
1 qt. cooked wild rice
1½ lbs. margarine
3-4 cups flour

In large saucepan cook chicken in about a gallon and a half chicken stock (or water) about 1 hour. Remove chicken, strain stock, and cool. Add celery, onions, and mushrooms. Simmer until vegetables are tender. In small saucepan melt margarine over low heat. Add flour slowly while cooking, stirring constantly until thickened to a heavy paste. Slowly add to chicken stock until thickened. Add chopped chicken and wild rice. Just before serving add cream and season with salt, white pepper, garlic, thyme, and Worcestershire Sauce. Serve hot. Makes about 2 gallons.

SAUERKRAUT KIELBASA SOUP

3-4 slices bacon diced
1 cup chopped onion
1 clove garlic, minced
1 lb. can sauerkraut, well drained
½ tsp. paprika
8 cups hot water
6 chicken bouillon cubes
3 cups peeled and diced potatoes
½ tsp. caraway seeds
⅛ tsp. pepper
1 lb. kielbasa, sliced
Parsley

In large kettle fry bacon until browned, add onion and garlic and saute for 3-4 minutes, stirring occasionally. Add sauerkraut, paprika, water, bouillon cubes, potatoes, caraway seeds, and pepper. Bring to a boil. Reduce heat and simmer, covered, for 20 minutes. Add kielbasa and simmer 15 minutes longer. Garnish with fresh parsley. About 3 quarts.

CHILLED PEACH SOUP

3 cups fresh peaches, pitted and sliced
2 cups yogurt
½ cup pineapple juice
1 cup orange juice
¼ cup lemon juice
1 cup peach nectar
2 cups sour cream
¼ cup sherry
½ cup non-dairy whipped topping

In blender add peaches, juice, sour cream, and sherry. Blend well, stir in whipped topping. Chill and serve in cold soup bowl. Garnish with mint leaf. Makes about 2 quarts.

FRENCH BREAD

1 pkg. dry yeast
2 cups lukewarm water, divided
2 tsp. salt
4 cups flour
1 Tbsp. sugar

Dissolve yeast in 1 cup water. In a large bowl, mix salt, flour, and sugar. Stir in yeast mixture and just enough of the second cup of water to hold dough together. Cover and let rise until double. Punch down and knead until smooth and elastic. Divide in half and shape into two long, thin loaves. Place on lightly greased foil-covered baking sheet. Slash loaves diagonally at 2-inch intervals. Bake at 375 degrees for 45 minutes. A pan of hot water on the oven shelf below will produce an extra good and crusty bread. Makes 2 loaves.

SWEDISH RYE BREAD

3 cups water, warm
1 Tbsp. salt
½ cup brown sugar
⅓ cup molasses
3 Tbsp. shortening
2 pkgs. yeast
1¼ cups rye flour
8-10 cups white flour, to make dough not sticky

Soak yeast in water until dissolved. Add sugar, molasses, salt, shortening, rye flour, and half of white flour and beat with rotary beater until smooth. Add flour until you can handle. Place on floured board and knead until smooth and elastic, about 5 to 10 minutes. Put in greased bowl and let rise until double. Punch down and let rise again. Form loaves and let rise until double. Bake at 375 degrees until done, approximately 30 minutes. About 3 loaves.

MORNING GLORY MUFFINS

2 cups flour
2 tsp. baking soda

½ tsp. salt
¾ tsp. cinnamon
1¼ cups sugar
¾ cup coconut
½ cup raisins
1 cup pecans
1 cup vegetable oil
3 eggs
½ tsp. vanilla
1½ cups finely shredded carrots
2 large apples, peeled, cored, and shredded

Preheat oven to 400 degrees. In large mixing bowl, combine flour, soda, salt, and cinnamon. Mix in sugar, coconut, raisins, and pecans. Add oil, eggs, and vanilla. Mix well and stir in apples and carrots. Spoon dough into paper-lined muffin tins, ¾ full, and bake for 30 minutes. Makes 2 dozen.

RUTTGER'S POTATO SALAD

5 lbs. cooked red potatoes, diced
2 cups chopped celery
2 cups chopped onion
2 cups sweet pickle relish
18 hard-cooked eggs, chopped
1 Tbsp. white pepper
½ cup salad mustard
2 cups brown sugar
1 cup cider vinegar
2 qts. salad dressing

In large bowl, put diced potatoes, celery, and onion. Add pickle relish, eggs, mustard and pepper. Toss lightly. Dissolve brown sugar with vinegar. Add salad dressing and whip until smooth. Pour over potato mixture and mix until all ingredients are coated. Refrigerate, covered, until serving time.

OPEN ROAD POTATOES

2 lbs. shredded hash browns
1¾ cups milk

1 cup Parmesan cheese
2 Tbsp. chopped chives
Dash white pepper
⅛ tsp. salt
¼ cup melted butter
Paprika

In large casserole dish, combine hash browns, Parmesan cheese, chives, salt, and pepper. Mix well. Pour milk over potatoes and drizzle butter on to potatoes. Sprinkle with paprika. Bake in oven at 375 degrees for 45 minutes. Serves 10-12.

LEMON CHICKEN

3 Tbsp. olive oil
4 (6 oz.) chicken breasts, boneless and skinless
1 tsp. chopped fresh parsley
½ tsp. dried whole thyme
¼ tsp. salt
1 cup white wine
3 Tbsp. lemon juice
¼ tsp. white pepper

Saute chicken breasts in oil in heavy skillet, cooking 5 minutes on each side. Place chicken in 8-inch baking dish, discarding drippings. Add parsley, thyme, and salt to wine; bring to a boil and pour over chicken. Sprinkle with lemon juice, pepper, and paprika. Cover and bake at 400 degrees for 20 minutes or until tender. Serves 4.

PAN FRIED WALLEYE

1 lb. walleye fillets
2 eggs
¼ cup milk
½ cup flour
½ cup cornmeal
1 tsp. salt
⅛ tsp. white pepper

In a small bowl, mix eggs and milk. In another flat bowl, combine dry ingredients.

Rinse fillets and pat dry. Sprinkle with flour, dip in egg mixture, then coat with dry ingredient mixture. Pan fry in heated 1/2 cup butter and 1/2 cup vegetable oil over medium heat until brown on both sides, turning once. 2-3 servings.

CANADIAN SHORELINE COD

2 lbs. boneless cod fillets
3 potatoes, peeled and sliced
3 carrots, peeled and sliced
1 medium onion, sliced
¼ lb. melted butter
2 Tbsp. seasoning salt
1 tsp. chopped, fresh parsley
⅛ tsp. white pepper

Place cod fillets in medium baking dish and sprinkle with half of salt. In medium saucepan, parboil potatoes and carrots in 3 cups of water, about 15 minutes. Drain, and layer over cod. Add sliced onions, drizzle with butter. Sprinkle with remaining salt and parsley. Cover and bake in 350 degree oven for 45 minutes. Serve immediately. Serves 4-6.

BETTE LE MAE

4 oz. semi-sweet chocolate
1⅓ cups sugar
2 oz. bitter chocolate
8 oz. butter
½ cup boiling water
5 whole eggs

Bring water and sugar to a rolling boil. Add chocolate and butter. Melt. Add eggs. Bake in a layer cake pan, 8- or 9-inch, lined with waxed paper on bottom. Bake at 350 degrees for 30 minutes in water bath. Cool. Remove from pan after 10 minutes. When completely cool, frost with glaze. GLAZE: Add 1½ cups chocolate chips to ½ cup scalded whipping cream, and stir until smooth.

Spread on desserts. Garnish with melted white chocolate.

CREME BRULEE

8 oz. brown sugar
12 egg yolks
6 oz. sugar
3 pints heavy cream, hot
1½ tsp. vanilla extract
¾ tsp. salt

Spread the brown sugar on a pan; dry out in a low oven. Cool, crush and sift. Mix together the egg yolks and granulated sugar until well-combined. Gradually stir in the hot cream. Add the vanilla and salt. Strain the mixture. Set 12 shallow ramekins or gratin dishes, about 1 inch deep, on a towel in a sheet pan (the purpose of the towel is to insulate the bottoms of the ramekins from the strong heat). Divide the custard mixture equally among the dishes. Pour into the sheet pan enough hot water to come about halfway up the sides of the ramekins. Bake at 350 degrees until the custard is just set, about 25 minutes. Cool, then refrigerate. To finish, first dab any moisture from the tops of the custards. Sprinkle with an even layer of brown sugar. Caramelize the sugar under the broiler; place them very close to the heat so that the sugar caramelizes quickly before the custard warms up too much (alternatively, use a blow torch). When it cools, the caramelized sugar will form a thin, hard crust. Serve within an hour or two. If the custards are held too long, the carmel tops will soften. Serves 12 portions, about 5 oz. each.

GREEK PASTA SALAD

Dressing:
1 cup olive oil
3 Tbsp. cider vinegar
2 Tbsp. chopped green onion

2 Tbsp. grated Parmesan cheese
2 tsp. basil leaves
½ tsp. salt
¼ tsp. pepper
¼ tsp oregano leaves

Salad:
8 oz. tri-colored rotini (corkscrew pasta)
2 small bell peppers, 1 red and 1 green, cut into ¼ inch strips
1 medium tomato, cut into 8 wedges
1 cup crumbled feta cheese
½ cup whole pitted ripe olives

Cook pasta as directed on package until el dente state -- DO NOT OVERCOOK or pasta will break apart in salad. Rinse with cold water, drain well. To hold pasta, coat with small amount of oil; cover and refrigerate. In blender container or food processor bowl with metal blade, combine all dressing indredients. Cover; blend or process until smooth; set aside. In large bowl combine all salad ingredients. Pour dressing over salad; toss gently to combine. Refrigerate at least 1 hour to blend flavors. Garnish with whole pitted ripe olives and red pepper strips. Yield: 5 cups.

RUTTGER'S 1000 ISLAND DRESSING
½ cup sugar
1 tsp. salt
1 qt. salad dressing
6 hard boiled eggs, chopped
½ cup chopped green pepper
½ cup pimento, chopped
¼ cup dried onion
¼ cup ketchup
¼ tsp. white pepper

Mix well and refrigerate in tightly covered container. Yields about ½ gallon.

RUTTGER'S GRANOLA
1 lb. 5 oz. quick oats
6 oz. wheat germ
1 cup sliced almonds
1 cup raisins
1 tsp. ground cinnamon
½ tsp. ground nutmeg
½ cup honey
½ cup brown sugar

In large mixing bowl mix oatmeal, wheat germ, almonds, brown sugar, cinnamon, and nutmeg until well blended. Bake on a couple of cookie sheets at 300 degrees about 1/2 hour, mixing twice. Let cool slightly, then add raisins and honey. Mix well. Store in tightly covered until ready to use.

APPLE OATMEAL COOKIES
1½ cups quick oats
¾ cup all purpose flour
¾ cup whole wheat flour
½ cup brown sugar, firmly packed
1 Tbsp. baking powder
¼ tsp. baking soda
½ tsp. salt
1½ tsp. cinnamon
½ cup raisins
1 cup Granny Smith apples, peeled and finely chopped
1 egg, slightly beaten
½ cup honey
½ cup oil
⅓ cup milk

Preheat oven to 375 degrees. In medium bowl combine oats, flours, brown sugar, baking soda, baking powder, salt, and cinnamon. Stir to combine. Stir in raisins and apples. In large bowl combine eggs, honey, oil, and milk. Stir in dry ingredients and mix to form a smooth batter. Drop batter onto paper-lined cookie sheet, using a small

scoop or rounded teaspoon about 2 inches apart. Dip finger into water and press dough down to about 1½ inch diameter. Bake for 10 minutes, and cool. Makes about 3 dozen.

CAFE LATTÉ RHUBARB PECAN CAKE

    1⅓ cups brown sugar
    ⅔ cup oil
    2 eggs
    1 tsp. vanilla
    1 cup buttermilk
    2⅔ cups flour
    ½ tsp. salt
    1 tsp. baking soda
    1 tsp. cinnamon
    2½ cups chopped rhubarb

Cream together brown sugar and oil. Scrape the bowl, add eggs, vanilla, and buttermilk. Combine flour, salt, baking soda and cinnamon. Mix well with sugar mixture. Fold in rhubarb. Divide batter between the two pans and spread out evenly. Bake 30 to 40 minutes. Cool in pans for 15 minutes. Frosting:

    1½ (8 oz.) pkgs. cream cheese, cold
    ¾ cups powdered sugar
    3 cups heavy whipping cream
    1 Tbsp. cinnamon
    2 Tbsp. maple syrup
    2 cups toasted ground pecans

Beat cold cream cheese and powdered sugar until smooth. Scrape the sides and bottom of mixing bowl. While mixer is beating, add whipping cream one cup at a time (not whipped) slowly, never allowing mixture to get too runny. Scrape bowl after each cup has been added. After all cream has been added and resembles whipped cream, add cinnamon and maple syrup. Beat only long enough to evenly distribute flavor through out frosting. To frost: Place one cake layer, top side down on cake platter. Put about 1 ½ cups frosting on layer and spread it evenly on top only. Place second layer, top side up, on the frosted layer. Frost sides of cake. The rest of the frosting goes on top. Frosting should be about one-half inch thick on top. Press the toasted ground pecans into the sides of the cake and sprinkle the rest of the nuts on top. Makes 12 to 16 servings.

ITALIAN CHEESECAKE

Crust:
    1¼ cups graham cracker crumbs
    ¼ cup sugar
    ½ tsp. cinnamon
    ⅓ cup butter

Mix above ingredients and press onto bottom of a 9-inch spring form pan.
Cheesecake:
    2 (15 or 16 oz.) containers of
        Ricotto cheese
    1 (14 oz.) Eagle Brand sweetened condensed milk
    4 eggs
    1 Tbsp. vanilla
    2 tsp. grated orange rind
    2 Tbsp. chopped candied cherries
    3 Tbsp. golden raisins
    1 Tbsp. flour

Beat Ricotta cheese and milk until smooth. Add eggs, vanilla, and orange rind. Mix well. In small bowl toss cherries, raisins, and flour to coat, then add to cheese mixture. Mix well. Pour into pan. Bake 1 hour and 10 minutes in 350 dgree preheated oven. Garnish with confectioners sugar and cinnamon. Yields 1 cake.

Dining Room Service

Many people have served in the dining room over the years. Sometimes people will come into the resort and tell how they worked in our dining room when they were  young, and that it was a very memorable time in their lives as there was fun along with the work. In the <u>American Resort</u> magazine of July 1929, there was an article about Ruttger's Lodge. It said the resort had a hostess for evening entertainment who also inspected the dining room and cabins to see that they were in order.

Ruby Treloar.

The best-known person connected with Ruttger's dining room is Ruby Treloar who has worked here since 1941. Ruby is known by many guests from old-timers right up to the present-day people. She is one of a kind in that she remembers people by name, when their birthdays are, and what type of food they prefer. She sends around 250 Christmas cards to guests and keeps in contact with those who are no longer able to come to Ruttger's due to health problems. Ruby has been known through all the years for her phenomenal memory. For instance, Barbara Smyers, a

guest for over 50 years, remembered when she was small she liked an ice cube in her milk. One year she missed coming to the resort, but when she returned the following year she came into the dining room and Ruby had an ice cube in her glass of milk.

Ruby calls herself a "little country girl," and she has been an amazing ambassador of good will for Ruttger's Bay Lake Lodge during all the years she has worked here. The Ruttger family all consider Ruby as a member of the family and have been so grateful for all the years they have been privileged to work with her and to call her a special friend. A typical occurrence: a long-time guest calls and says "I haven't been

Ruby—well-known dining room hostess at Ruttger's Bay Lake Lodge.

American Hotel & Motel Association Employee of the Year- 1995

54-year hostess awarded national employee honor

By Robert Franklin
Staff Writer

When Ruby Treloar left home Monday, about 10 neighbors formed a car caravan at 6:15 a.m. to escort her out of Aitkin County, Minn.

It's not every day a friend goes to Atlanta to be named the Outstanding Lodging Employee of the Year by the American Hotel & Motel Association.

Treloar, 74, has worked at Ruttger's Bay Lake Lodge north of Garrison, Minn., since 1941, first as a waitress and then for about 20 years as a hostess. "I went to help them for a few days, and a few days turned into 54 years," she said Wednesday. Guests recalled her as the 4-foot-11 waitress who could remember large orders without writing them down.

But that's only part of her story. "I keep a great correspondence with a lot of the guests, too," she said. "They're my family away from home." Her boss, owner Jack Ruttger, said she sends Christmas cards and writes to about 250 of the lodge's regular guests. She also brings flowers from her garden for the lodge's dining tables, visits friends in nursing homes and drives elderly neighbors on errands. She can speak Norwegian and, until about five years ago, used to do a lot of ice fishing. She also runs her own five-cabin resort on Farm Island Lake, where she lives in the house in which she was born.

The association, which represents more than 10,000 hotels, motels and resorts, will give Treloar a plaque, $1,000 and a seven-day expense-paid trip for two anywhere in the

Ruby Treloar

continental United States. Her destination is undecided, she said. She has no plans to retire, she said, "unless they fire me." Not much chance of that, according to Ruttger. "When they come," he said, "they ask for Ruby. They don't ask for any of us."

Reprint from the newspaper.

there for 25 years. What's changed? Tell me, is Ruby still there?" No mention of a Ruttger! We truly love Ruby as so many of our guests do.

My Long-Term Connection with Ruttger's –by Ruby Treloar

In the early 1940s, I was vacationing at my home on Farm Island Lake when my husband, Bill, and I were living in New York. One day I was entertaining my ladies club and got a knock on the door. It was Alec Ruttger out looking for help. My girl-friend, Mayme Geyer, was there with me

and she said "Let's Go!" I had planned to go back to New York, but I had a little time to spare so I said I would go and talk to Alec. I remember telling Mayme that we didn't know much about doing that kind of work, as we would be working with rich people and were only little country farm girls. We went to talk to Alec that evening. He told us his brother, Max, needed help at Pine Beach Lodge on Gull Lake more than he did at Bay Lake so if we could work there it would be appreciated. I had the car, and Mayme talked me into going to work at Pine Beach the next day, and that is when

we met Aunt Rosie Ruttger. When Pine Beach closed in the fall, Alec asked me to finish out the season at Bay Lake as one of the girls that had been waitressing had fallen and hurt her back. I had planned to return to New York, but my husband called and told me that he was returning to Minnesota. I told Alec I would work for a few days more–and that is what has turned out to be more than 50 years!

When I started, there were seven waitresses in the dining room, and I was called head waitress. This meant planning the daily duties for waitresses and table assignments for guests.

One time, when I had first started at Bay Lake, I went to one of my guest tables with pad and pencil to get the order, and the young boy in the family looked up at me and said, "Our waitress before you never wrote anything down. She remembered!" That impressed me greatly so I decided I could do that too. After that, I remembered all orders and could remember from year to year special requests from regular guests, and I surprised them with my memory.

The years went by, with dining room staff working three meals per day, with one evening off each week; one half of the employees on Friday evening and the other half on Sunday evening as they served buffet those two evenings. We polished silverware every morning before breakfast.

Then the resort grew and started catering to conventions. I became more involved in hostessing and less with waiting on tables. In 1982, I won a contest for "Employee of the Year" in Minnesota. I was awarded a $100 savings bond and a trip to the St. James Hotel in Red Wing. Another year I won the WCCO Good Neighbor Award. In 1995, I won the competition as the National Outstanding Hospitality Employee of the Year, given out by the American Hotel and Motel Association Annual Convention in Atlanta, Georgia. I received $1,000 cash and a trip to Hawaii as my prize. In October of 1995, I was chosen to go to Washington D.C. for the first White House Tourism Conference where I met President Clinton and Vice President Gore. In October of 1996, I received the Hospy Award.

I worked for Ruttger's at Marathon Shores on the Florida Keys during the winters from 1968 to 1980 returning to Bay Lake to work summers.

Children's Supervision and Entertainment

The first mention of children's supervision I have found was in a 1934 spring newsletter. The statement was made that Miss Palmer would be back again that year. I would guess that was the second year for such a position. I do remember Della Mullen, who is pictured with Jane Ruttger and Gretchen Klein probably at the age of three—which would make that about 1937. She worked in the summers with just board and lodging as her pay.

Jane Ruttger Bobich reminisced about the playground activity program. She said that Della Mullin was a playground "girl" in the late 1930s. There were no planned activities like Kids' Kamp has now. The playground was located in front of the first circle of cabins east of the lodge. Dorothy Morrison came to us in the late 1940s. She was a college student from Oklahoma. As there began to be more guests, and of course more children, there was a need for more than one playground girl.

Gretchen Klein and Jane Bobich with Kim Sirridge, Kansas City, Kansas, 1995. Kim Sirridge is a fourth-generation guest, her great-grandfather, Dr. Earl Joss, first visited Ruttger's in the early 1900s.

Della Mullin pictured with Gretchen Klein, Sharon Crow, and Jane Ruttger Bobich, 1939.

By the 1950s, the playground was moved to a spot by the lake where boats are kept now. An outdoor pool was added, and children were supervised at the playground, pool, and the beach. In case of bad weather they were taken to the lobby area.

Barb Simons arrived in 1956, with her mother, Lucia, and brother, Joe. She worked on the playground for several years.

Kids' Kamp began in 1987 with Edie Rue as the director. Safe new equipment was added to the playground which was then located on the present location on the hill west of the villas. As is always true, a resort must be updated and improved upon in all areas, as there are always new ideas and types of equipment being developed that will make more comfortable and enjoyable vacations for guests.

Kids' Kamp, for many years known as the playground, has been a mainstay of our summer offering to families. It gives Mom and Dad a little break to do what they want to do. It takes a crew of six to run the program today.

Molly, Julie, and Blake Platisha on the beach.

The Simons Family at Ruttger's

Lucia Simons.

In the fall of 1955, Lucia Simons and her two children, Joe and Barbara, moved to Brainerd where Lucia had accepted a position at the Harrison Elementary School as a kindergarten teacher. During that year, she noticed an ad in the Brainerd paper that Ruttger's was looking for a dining room hostess. After meeting with Alec and Jack over coffee at a local restaurant, she was hired. That summer the three of them moved out to the resort with Lucia and Barb staying in the "hen house" and Joe in the busboy shack. At that time, Joe was 13 and Barb was 11. Joe helped in the dining room pouring coffee and busing dishes, and Barb was a baby-sitter for Jack and Ann's children—first Sandy and then Julie the next summer.

During the 11 summers Lucia worked at the resort, she became known for her

Playground director Barb Simons on the diving board, 1962.

jovial manner and fun parties. She will be remembered for the Saturday night hat parties, the card tournaments which sometimes lasted until midnight or later, the Bingo calling, Christmas in July celebrations, the style shows' emcee as the "Lolli Pop Lady," and as the popular Saturday water show emcee.

Joe was quite a skier. He, along with Jack Ruttger, also an excellent skier, did a clown act "encouraging" anyone else they could find to join in. Those two dressed up as women were a big hit! They, along with Joanie Anderson, did a pyramid ski act for many years. Other skiers remembered were Jane Johnson, Chi Chi Butorac, Joanie Vaughn, and the boat driver Harvey Throop. Barb did an act on the trampoline and later organized a group of girls to do a synchronized swimming act in the pool. She first worked with Mary Ochsner and later with Debbie and Pam Bobich, daughters of Jane Ruttger Bobich, and with Julie Ruttger. Barb recalled that Myrle Ruttger had made tutus of nylon net for them to wear in their act.

Joe met Sharon Boyum at Moorhead State College, and they were married in 1967. Joe was teaching and coaching at Gary, Minnesota, at that time, and Sharon was teaching art in Moorhead. In the summer of 1969, they came back to Ruttgers to run the golf and gift shop which was located in the present Auntie M's building (formerly Corner Sportswear). The seasons then were Memorial Day to Labor Day, so it worked out well for teachers. Joe operated the golf shop until the resort season

Trish, Chad, Erika, Joe, and Sharon Simons.

stretched to six or seven months, which interfered with his school job. Joe has worked on the golf course part-time since then.

The gift shop had depended on traveling vendors for goods until Sharon discovered markets in the Twin Cities for gift ware and clothing and began expanding both for sale in the shop. In 1977, the gifts were moved into the Country Store, and the golf shop expanded with sportswear, carrying golf and tennis clothing along with traditional sports apparel. The golf shop was moved across the highway in 1987, and the building on the corner became known as

Kay Gaudette and Sharon Simons.

Putter & Putt, now Auntie M's Kaffeehaus.

the Corner Sportswear.

All three of the Simons' children have worked for the resort during their high school and college years. Chad worked in the golf shop and Trish and Erika worked in the sportswear and gift shops. Trish still attends markets on occasion.

Sharon and her friend, Kay Gaudette, have worked together in the stores for 12 summers and have traveled to many markets to stock the shops with specialty clothing, gifts, and decorative items. They also have taken on the task of organizing the popular Oktoberfest arts and crafts fair.

The Corner Sportswear building (formerly the Paul Bunyan Trading Post, the Golf Shop, the Putter & Putt Shop) has been renamed again. In 1997, it was remodeled to become a coffee, espresso, bagel, pizza, and ice cream shop. It features Ruttger memorabilia on the walls and has a feeling of the 1950s, when it was built. The new name is Auntie M's Kaffeehaus, after Mae Ruttger Heglund, Jack's sister, who operated the shop before she was married. ℛ

Grand opening, Auntie M's Kaffeehaus, June 1997. L to R: Mary Witchger, Ann Ruttger, Laura and Mae Heglund, Buzz and Jack Ruttger.

Mae Heglund; Greg Meyer, director of sales and decorating coordinator; and Sharon Simons at the grand opening.

Chapter Thirteen

Ruttger's Guests are Ruttger Friends

The Family Type of Business —*by Jack Ruttger*

With the extension of the season from Memorial Day through Labor Day, to Easter through November 1st, the resort has expanded its market to include the convention/conference business, primarily in April, May, June, September, and October. The comment we receive from most folks is "what a great family atmosphere you have!" That, my dear friends, is not by accident. We were started by Grandpa and Grandma, Joe and Josie Ruttger, and their four Ruttger sons doing everything to service their few guests at the start. From that very, very humble beginning when Josie did all of the cooking and Joe and

Dr. Carl Kohlbry, Duluth, Minnesota, his family were guests for many years.

the boys did all of the maintenance, fish cleaning, yard work, and kitchen work, there have been Ruttgers in the kitchen, in the dining room, cleaning fish, at the front desk, and in general there to make sure that a family tradition is carried on. Our motto is: "Feels Like Family."

What started as a family serving families in 1898, is still true today. As the oldest resort in Minnesota under the ownership of one family, it still has the Ruttger family serving members of families who were with us at the turn of that century. Billy Aye, of the F. I. Boone family from 1899, is still a sometime visitor and a

The Boones from Manhattan, Kansas, 1925.

Dr. and Mrs. Harry Klein –Duluth, Minnesota, 1949.

very close friend. Gretchen Klein has been a continuous guest since her third birthday and has had every birthday here since 1937. Her father, Dr. Harry Klein of Duluth, first vacationed at Ruttger's with his family in 1912. Lloyd Kolliner, formerly of Stillwater, Minnesota, began his vacations at Bay Lake with his family in 1925 and continued staying here until his death in 1978.

In 1922, Elsie and Dr. John McNutt honeymooned at Ruttger's. They virtually raised their children with us and very often enjoyed their anniversary here, too. The celebrations were many and included their 50th and 60th wedding anniversaries at Ruttger's. Dr. McNutt passed on in 1983, but Elsie came with her family as a reunion group almost every year after that up through the summer of 1996—she even

Dr. and Mrs. John McNutt –Duluth, Minnesota.

played golf that summer! At the age of 95, Elsie McNutt passed away in December of 1996.

There have been other families that have followed the same tradition. A family would practically raise their children at Bay Lake on summer vacations—then, like the McNutts, when the children grew up and had families of their own, a custom would start of setting aside vacation time each summer for everyone to get together.

Jim and Henriette Klingel vacationed with their children Steve, Laura, Cindy, and Todd starting back in the early 1950s. They haven't missed a year. Jim has passed away, and Henny is now married to Robert Johnsen, and the whole gang, usually around 20, comes every year as the Klingel/Johnsen family reunion.

The Ritchie clan—Wichita, Kansas, early 1930s. See next page.

The Ritchie family from Wichita, Kansas, was among our early regular guests. Following is a poem that appeared in several of our very earliest brochures written by Mrs. C. A. (Aimee) Ritchie:

"Oh, meet us at Bay Lake, in June and
    July,
The time quickly passes, the months will
    soon fly.
Clean up your golf clubs as bright as can be,
And meet us at Ruttger's on the first tee.
Keep the moths out of your best bathing
    suit,
Get yourself set for a regular "toot."
And in the cool evenings we'll visit and
    sing,
And oh what a pleasure these friendships
    will bring.
For friends like you are the very best sort—
So meet us in June at Ruttger's Resort."

We have mentioned just a few of the long-term family friends of the resort. There are dozens and dozens more, and each year we add to the list.

We like to feel that it is our family form of operation that makes us special to the wonderful family trade we have developed. When a Ruttger still active in the resort operation can have known and greeted four generations, who vacationed together through the years—and especially when that Ruttger served the first generation—then that is something special!!

Dave Ritchie, Wichita, Kansas, 1928, on Ruttger's sand green.

Our Tree   *—by Gretchen Klein*

Some may stop by the tree in person. Others may see the tree in their imaginations during a moment of remembering. Our tree, a pine, is located near the entrance of Ruttger's. The plaque beneath the tree reminds all guests that they are "The treasured and faithful friends."

Our tree stands as a symbol of those who have vacationed on Bay Lake during the first one hundred years of the resort. In its needles, branches, trunk, and roots are the stored memories of events and friends that thousands have experienced at the spot we call Ruttger's. Though our tree represents one hundred years of guests, it is appropriate that our tree is a relatively young pine. The past, no matter its length or glory, is but prologue for today and tomorrow.

Look closely at the pine tree. Think of each needle as a guest. Some are new this year, yet already securely attached. Some of the needles represent guests who have been Ruttger regulars for five, ten, twenty, or more years. Some needles represent guests who first came to Ruttger's over fifty years ago. Often they are a part of a family with a history dating back eighty, ninety, or more years. The needles on the ground represent those guests no longer with us. Each of them contributed to the family resort we now enjoy.

Note the branches that support the needles. The oldest branches are the first guests from the Twin Cities, Duluth, Kansas, and Illinois. Other branches represent a variety of states and countries. Each branch originally contained but a few needles and has grown dramatically over the years. Look at the branches again and this time think of them in time periods. There is a branch of

Ann Ruttger, Gretchen Klein, and Jack Ruttger, Oktoberfest, 1996. Gretchen Klein has become a great friend through the many years she's been a guest at Ruttger's Bay Lake Lodge. She has spent every birthday here since 1937. Her father, Dr. Harry Klein, first visited in 1912. She is seen here planting "Our Tree," October 19, 1996.

traditional Memorial Day guests, one for the Fourth of July, another branch represents the first week of August, and surely one branch the guests of Oktoberfest.

The trunk of our tree supports the branches and needles as it brings nourishment from the roots. The trunk is a unique combination of owners, staff, and guests that defines a Ruttger vacation.

Viewing the roots of our tree is accomplished through pictures and words. We were not here at the beginning, and only a few of us have had the privilege of knowing all four generations of Ruttgers who have owned and operated this special place on the north shore of Bay Lake. Each year brings changes, be they small or large. Yet, each year is exactly the same as the years gone by—only better.

The pine tree, like the resort, will continue to grow in the second hundred years. The roots of the Ruttger family are strong and deep. The trunk of the Ruttgers, staff, and guests is sturdy and straight. The branches will continue to expand. Individual needles, the guests, will age and fall, and new ones will take their places. This is our tree. We are the guests of Ruttger's Bay Lake Lodge.

Many thanks to Gretchen for writing "Our Tree," which is a part of a speech she gave. She represented our guests who have stayed with us through these many years. ℛ

Christmas card 1956, Alec and Sandy Ruttger. Each year a tree is planted in honor of someone important to Ruttger's Bay Lake Lodge at our Oktoberfest celebration. In 1997, we honored Alexander John (Sandy) Ruttger III, 1954-1973. In 1998, the honor goes to Joseph and Josie Ruttger and Alec and Myrle Ruttger.

Chapter Fourteen
Ruttger's Today

Ruttger's Today

—by Chris Ruttger

Much has changed here in the 30 some years I can remember. In the 70s and 80s many small resorts went out of business, selling their valuable, and heavily taxed, lakeshore property for residential use. There was a sense among resorters that you had to grow or die. With 40 cottages, full-service dining, a golf course, and other services, we were certainly a bigger operation than many. Still, it seemed our future was uncertain if we didn't keep moving.

The greatest growth came in the early 80s when we tripled in capacity over a four-year period. With finance specialist, Perry Platisha (my brother-in-law), and sales and marketing specialist, Fred Bobich (my cousin), Dad built and sold 88 condominium units. In the following years, they added 12 more villa units and a championship nine-hole golf course, which expanded in 1992 to become *The Lakes*, our 18-hole course. Today we have 168 accommodations with room for up to 350 people.

The first State Farm group who met here in the 50s sat on wooden benches in Paul Bunyan Hall which doubled as a recreation building. When we built the first conference center in 1971, many meeting groups tried us for the first time, and their response was overwhelming. The new facility was fine, but they loved the personal attention, service, and food we offered. They came back, they told their friends, and the conference business grew. We expanded the conference facilities in 1985 to 10,000 square feet of meeting and banquet space, and the conference business allowed us to expand our season from four to seven months.

From the beginning, we have been known for food, service, and friendliness. As we grew and reached out to new markets, we found that people expected a little more. We needed to become a little more professional, which is not to say commercial; we did not want to lose our family feel. Our staff has increased from fewer than 100 in 1977 to 300 in 1997. I remember my parents' first steps to hand over a little responsibility to a couple of assistants. Now nine full-time department heads, an administrative assistant, and a controller make up our administrative team. Among them are veterans Sharon Simons, who started in 1969 (see page 128); Al Cunningham, who started in 1979; and Terry Dox, who started in 1984.

Al started in the grounds department when the concept of a separate grounds crew was a new thing. Dad realized we had a beautiful spot, and in the 70s he decided it was time to make the most of it. He made landscaping a priority and brought in an educated professional to make it happen. Al's influence was apparent his first season here, and it has been ever since. Today, Al controls the grounds, property, and housekeeping departments. His staff of five gardeners and four groundskeepers display 50,000 annuals and perennials and have planted over 800 trees and shrubs.

Terry, also known as Chef Dox or simply Chef, probably did not know what he was getting into when he moved here from St. Paul in 1984. He took on the challenge of continuing the reputation earned by Grandma Josie, Amy and Bertha, and others. It was a reputation for excellent food that was lauded by Duncan Hines as early as 1940 and enjoyed by generations of

Ruttger's guests. He proved to be up to the challenge in every way. With a cooperative, whatever-it-takes attitude (not typical of chefs), he produced consistently flavorful food. About the time Terry arrived, we built a new kitchen and turned the old kitchen into an additional dining room. His ability to meet the challenge as we have grown, as tastes have changed, and as our guests' expectations have elevated, is a credit to his talents and abilities.

Lately the administrative team has been brushing up on our family history in a series of retreats. The goal is to align ourselves with each other and with the values that have allowed Ruttger's to prosper. My parents have spent several sessions telling stories and answering questions, and we now have a time line that starts in 1880. Sifting through history, searching for the values and aspirations that drove previous generations, has been enlightening. The foundation has been there all along, and articulating our mission and our guiding principles has already made decisions about our future clearer.

Jack and Chris on the deck overlooking Bay Lake.

Ruttger Family Tree

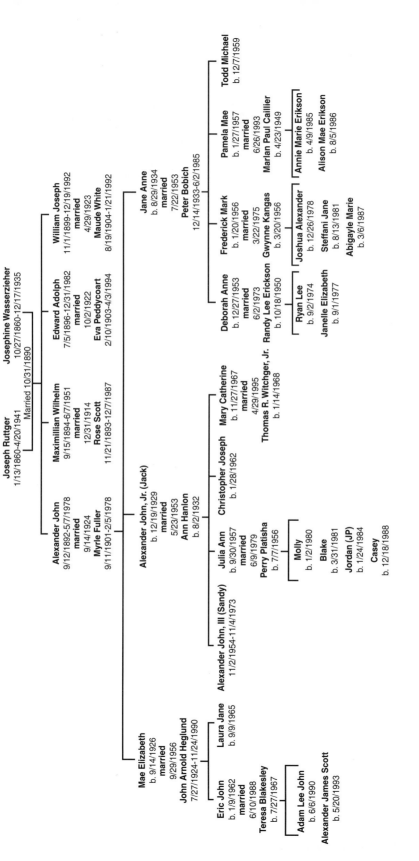

Joseph Ruttger
1/13/1860-4/20/1941

Josephine Wasserzieher
10/27/1860-12/17/1935

Married 10/31/1890

Alexander John
9/12/1892-5/7/1978
married
9/14/1924
Myrtle Fuller
9/11/1901-2/5/1978

Maximillian Wilhelm
9/15/1894-6/7/1951
married
12/31/1914
Rose Scott
11/21/1893-12/7/1987

Edward Adolph
7/5/1896-12/31/1982
married
10/2/1922
Eva Peddycoart
2/10/1903-4/3/1994

William Joseph
11/1/1899-12/19/1992
married
4/29/1923
Maude White
8/19/1904-1/21/1992

Jane Anne
b. 8/29/1934
married
7/22/1953
Peter Bobich
12/14/1933-6/2/1985

Todd Michael
b. 12/7/1959

Pamela Mae
b. 1/27/1957
married
6/26/1993
Marlan Paul Caillier
b. 4/23/1949

Annie Marie Erikson
b. 4/9/1985

Alison Mae Erikson
b. 8/5/1986

Frederick Mark
b. 1/20/1956
married
3/22/1975
Gwynne Kangas
b. 3/20/1956

Deborah Anne
b. 11/27/1953
married
6/2/1973
Randy Lee Erickson
b. 10/18/1950

Joshua Alexander
b. 12/26/1978

Steffani Jane
b. 8/13/1981

Abigayle Marie
b. 3/6/1987

Ryan Lee
b. 9/2/1974

Janelle Elizabeth
b. 9/1/1977

Mae Elizabeth
b. 9/14/1926
married
9/29/1956
John Arnold Heglund
7/27/1924-11/24/1990

Alexander John, Jr. (Jack)
b. 12/19/1929
married
5/23/1953
Ann Hanlon
b. 8/2/1932

Christopher Joseph
b. 1/28/1962

Mary Catherine
b. 11/27/1967
married
4/29/1995
Thomas R. Witchger, Jr.
b. 1/14/1968

Laura Jane
b. 9/9/1965

Alexander John, III (Sandy)
11/2/1954-11/4/1973

Julia Ann
b. 9/30/1957
married
6/9/1979
Perry Platisha
b. 7/7/1956

Molly
b. 1/2/1980

Blake
b. 3/31/1981

Jordan (JP)
b. 1/24/1984

Casey
b. 12/18/1988

Eric John
b. 1/9/1962
married
6/10/1988
Teresa Blakesley
b. 7/27/1967

Adam Lee John
b. 6/6/1990

Alexander James Scott
b. 5/20/1993

Color Photos

Some Things Feel Just Like Family

Year after year, decade after decade, relationships are made that last. There is a feeling of family for the people who are pictured on the following pages. This is a presentation of the long-time family groups. There are literally thousands more who could be shown. With these pictures and their captions, we hope to give you an overview of the relationships we have with people. There has always been a Ruttger involved in the day-to-day operation, and this has ensured a bonding with our guests. The motto of our resort is "Feels Like Family."

Faithful friends for nearly 40 years. Seated (left to right): Lucille Brewster, Salina, Kansas; Dallas and Wanda Perry, Eau Claire, Wisconsin. Standing (left to right): George and Connie Johnson, Salina, Kansas; Jack and Ann Ruttger; Virginia and Elmer Ridgeway, Oklahoma City, Oklahoma.

Bob and Henriette Johnsen of St. Paul, Minnesota, and the Klingel family. Three generations. They have been coming every year since the 1950s.

▲ West Central State Farm Insurance group from Lincoln, Nebraska. First group to meet at Ruttger's. Date of that meeting was in the early 1950s. Now, as retirees, they meet at Ruttger's in late August. Note Ann Ruttger on Jack's lap and Ruby Treloar sitting on the deck.

◄ Jim and Mary Hokanson of Marigold Foods have entertained several groups of clients here every summer for many years. Jim is proud of his handicap on the golf course, which is in the low single digits.

A fun time with old friends in the 50s. Seated: ▶ Carl Dahms. Front Row (left to right): Ann Ruttger, Lucille Hollister, Alex Klein, Peg Dahms, Grace Kampmeier. Back row: Jack Ruttger, Darrell Hollister, Ruttger's guest, Ethel Ekstrom, Mrs. Larry Wolfe, Fred Kampmeier, and Dr. Harry Klein. Dr. Klein first visited Ruttger's in 1912. The other guests started coming in the mid to late 1930s and never missed a year, even during the war.

Judge Harry Thomas pictured, and his wife Edith, of Kansas City, Missouri, spent four weeks every summer until he passed away in the 70s. He loved to fish. Ruby Treloar, our dining room hostess since 1941, would find Judge Harry a local boy to row for him each summer. The most noted boat rower was Bobby Olson, 15 years old and very Swedish. To Judge Thomas the boat rower was Mr. Olson, to Bobby Olson the Judge was just plain Harry.

▲ Frank and Luella Smyers (seated) and their daughters Barbara and Shirley from Munster, Indiana, vacationed in the 40s and every year after. Seated, from left: Luella Smyers, Todd Carley, and Frank Smyers. Standing, from left: Ruby Treloar, Dane Carley, Shirley Carley, John Carley, and Barb Rybicki. Frank passed away late in 1996, and daughter, Barb, in early 1997. Luella, Shirley, and the boys returned to Bay Lake in the summer of 1997.

▲ Norma and Gene Peterson from Illinois. Gene is a childhood friend of Jack Ruttger and was an employee in the mid-40s. The parents of Gene and Jack were very close friends. Gene was Ruby's favorite busboy, and there have been 57 summers worth of busboys for Ruby to supervise and scold.

Meet our Family

Jack and Ann Ruttger Family ▶
First Row: Jordan, Molly, and Blake Platisha.
Second Row: Ann Ruttger, Casey Platisha,
Jack Ruttger. Third Row: Mary Ruttger
Witchger, Tom Witchger, Chris Ruttger,
Perry Platisha, Julia Ruttger Platisha.

▲ Pete and Jane Bobich Family
Standing: Gwynne Bobich, Deb Erickson, Marlan Caillier, Pam Caillier, Fred Bobich, Josh
Bobich, Todd Bobich, Janelle Erickson, Randy Erickson. Front Row: Steffani Bobich, Jane
Ruttger Bobich, Alison Erikson, Ryan Erickson, Abigayle Bobich, Annie Erikson.

Pete Bobich (deceased).

▲ John and Mae Heglund Family
Laura Jane Heglund, Mae Ruttger Heglund, John Arnold
Heglund (deceased), and Eric Heglund.

▲ Eric and Teresa Heglund Family
Teresa, Eric, Adam, Alexander.

◄ Julia Ruttger Platisha,
Molly and Blake, 1983.

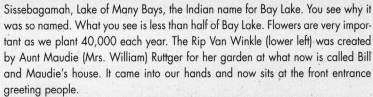

Sissebagamah, Lake of Many Bays, the Indian name for Bay Lake. You see why it was so named. What you see is less than half of Bay Lake. Flowers are very important as we plant 40,000 each year. The Rip Van Winkle (lower left) was created by Aunt Maudie (Mrs. William) Ruttger for her garden at what now is called Bill and Maudie's house. It came into our hands and now sits at the front entrance greeting people.

The dining room overlooking Bay Lake. The "Old Log" dining room was built in 1922 (center with the gable roof). The addition to the left was added on in 1987.

Early morning sunrise.

The joy of summer. Thousands have learned to water ski at Ruttger's.

A stroll on the beach before the kids launch the playak boats. The sunfish and crappies always bite while fishing from the dock. Occasionally, a bass or northern pike will strike the bait as well.

Hole No. 5, 512 Yards, Par 5 on The Lakes.

A view of the 18th green on The Lakes from the clubhouse deck.

The second hole tee box on the Lodge Nine.

#17 green, with Bass Lake in the background. Par 4, 372 yards.

Reception lobby. Pictures on the wall are: 1890 wedding portrait of pioneers Joe and Josie Ruttger, 1924 wedding portrait of Alec and Myrle Ruttger, and an early photograph of the four Ruttger boys with their father, Joe. The antique furniture is from Aunt Maudie Ruttger's house.

Centennial Library. In honor of our 100 years.

Golf course condominiums.

Cottage interiors.

Flowers engulf the cottages.

Old Log Dining Room. Built in 1922 with local labor and local logs.

Chef Terry Dox, since 1984.

Lobby with split rock fireplace built in 1925.

Ruttger's Country Store. The store dates back to 1906, and has the original tin ceiling and hardwood floor.

From the old Ruttger house of 1898, currently the "corner stone" of our Lodge, Ruttger's has grown to 170 units, dining rooms to seat 300, and 27 holes of golf (the fenced in greens are gone). The staff at the turn of the century was family members. Now it numbers 300 in the summer. It has been a labor of love for three generations of Ruttger's, and now Christopher will add his "magical" touch. Old–timers will remember Chris' magic shows at the resort as a child. So expect some "hocus-pocus" during his reign.

Resort Committee of the American Hotel Association at Basin Harbor Resort, VT, 1994. Such resorts as the Greenbrier, WV; The Cloister, GA; Opryland, TN; Grand Hotel, MI; Broadmoor, CO; Banff Hotel, Alberta, Canada; Del Coronado, CA; Mauna Kea, HI; and Pebble Beach Lodge, CA are represented in this photo. Jack Ruttger, (left first row), is a long-time member that has just gone honorary, and Chris Ruttger has been elected to this 60-member committee. ℛ